T0358340

Cambridge Elements

Elements in Construction Grammar
edited by
Thomas Hoffmann
Catholic University of Eichstätt-Ingolstadt
Alexander Bergs
Osnabrück University

CONSTRUCTIONS AND COMPOSITIONALITY

Cognitive and Computational Explorations

Giulia Rambelli
University of Bologna

CAMBRIDGE
UNIVERSITY PRESS

Shaftesbury Road, Cambridge CB2 8EA, United Kingdom

One Liberty Plaza, 20th Floor, New York, NY 10006, USA

477 Williamstown Road, Port Melbourne, VIC 3207, Australia

314–321, 3rd Floor, Plot 3, Splendor Forum, Jasola District Centre, New Delhi – 110025, India

103 Penang Road, #05–06/07, Visioncrest Commercial, Singapore 238467

Cambridge University Press is part of Cambridge University Press & Assessment, a department of the University of Cambridge.

We share the University's mission to contribute to society through the pursuit of education, learning and research at the highest international levels of excellence.

www.cambridge.org
Information on this title: www.cambridge.org/9781009517393

DOI: 10.1017/9781009437929

First published 2024

A catalogue record for this publication is available from the British Library.

ISBN 978-1-009-51739-3 Hardback
ISBN 978-1-009-43796-7 Paperback
ISSN 2753-2674 (online)
ISSN 2753-2666 (print)

Constructions and Compositionality

Cognitive and Computational Explorations

Elements in Construction Grammar

DOI: 10.1017/9781009437929
First published online: November 2024

Giulia Rambelli
University of Bologna

Author for correspondence: Giulia Rambelli, giulia.rambelli4@unibo.it

Abstract: How do we understand any sentence, from the most ordinary to the most creative? The traditional assumption is that we rely on formal rules combining words (compositionality). However, psycho- and neurolinguistic studies point to a linguistic representation model that aligns with the assumptions of Construction Grammar: There is no sharp boundary between stored sequences and productive patterns. Evidence suggests that interpretation alternates compositional (incremental) and noncompositional (global) strategies. Accordingly, systematic processes of language productivity are explainable by analogical inferences rather than compositional operations: Novel expressions are understood "on the fly" by analogy with familiar ones. This Element discusses compositionality, alternative mechanisms in language processing, and explains why Construction Grammar is the most suitable approach for formalizing language comprehension.

This Element also has a video abstract: www.cambridge.org/EICG-Rambelli

Keywords: compositionality, analogy, language processing, Construction Grammar, computational modeling

JEL classifications: A12, B34, C56, D78, E90

ISBNs: 9781009517393 (HB) 9781009437967 (PB) 9781009437929 (OC)
ISSNs: 2753-2674 (online) 2753-2666 (print)

Contents

1 Introduction

Understanding and generating novel sentences is often considered the hallmark of human language. It is striking how, given a finite inventory of means, speakers can always process and produce new expressions through which they can convey a new trend, realize a poem, express emotions, or produce scientific theories. In that sense, language is a remarkable example of human creativity. Theories of language refer to this phenomenon as the *productivity* (sometimes named *creativity*) of language, and they usually explain this by the fact that language processing is driven by a mechanism that composes the meaning of words into larger semantic units to create novel combinations.

Nevertheless, the influence of context on the interpretation or generation of a sentence is equally characteristic of language understanding. People have a great deal of previous linguistic and extralinguistic experience they use to build rich, elaborated representations of texts and conversations. In each utterance or discourse, each word acts as a cue to "activate" and retrieve related background knowledge, creating anticipations (or expectations) about sentence completion. In a general sense, this trait could be designated as the *context-sensitivity* of language: Sentence comprehension results from how preexisting linguistic knowledge and contextual constraints combine to make a particular linguistic form.

The following examples illustrate these observations:

(1) a. *The child spilled the milk all over the floor.*
   b. *The child spilled the rice all over the floor.*

Both sentences are syntactically well-formed and generate meaningful semantic representation; that is, they are both semantically plausible. The first utterance includes nonnovel combinations of words: *Milk* is something we experienced to *spill* very often, and specifically, *spill the milk* is a chunk of words recurrent in texts. Usually, interpreting this kind of sentence eases the processing determined by several rationales (the expression is stored in long-term memory, the words match semantic expectations, etc.). Conversely, the situation reflected in the second sentence is unexpected. A comprehender could have never directly experienced that scene or heard this sequence of words (which is quite rare[1]). Therefore, interpreting this unusual utterance should rely on a specific process. While the classic mechanism proposed in the literature relies on a building-block strategy, where the final meaning is somehow built

---

[1] Observing the bigram frequencies in a large corpus of English – the enTenTen18 corpus (Jakubíček et al., 2013) – the word *milk* occurs as the object of the verb *spill* 2,392 times, while *spill * rice* occurs just 37 times.

from single utterance components, an alternative hypothesis is to characterize this process as a generalization based on similar previous experiences driven by other inference mechanisms (co-activated network of representations, analogical inferences, and so forth). Despite the vast amount of research in sentence processing offered by linguistic and psycholinguistic literature, it is still debatable how language users deal with the challenge of interpreting sentences presented in real time, incrementally, word by word. Accordingly, efforts are focused on formalizing a linguistic theory that can provide an adequate description and computational model of language processing.

This Element (1) proposes a review of what compositionality has been defined in general and its concrete transposition in different formalisms, (2) summarizes several experimental works that demolish (or largely downsize) the role of compositionality in language processing, (3) introduces analogy as a mechanism that could be used to build meaning, and (4) defines the role of compositionality in a usage-based constructionist perspective. In all cases, the theoretical perspectives, experimental data supporting these observations, and the potential applications to a computational model of language processing are presented.

From a broad perspective, the Element provides an overview of mechanisms proposed to explain language comprehension and their potential integration into a comprehensive theory of language processing. Before delving into specific details, the next section will introduce the two concurrent general mechanisms that linguistic theories have posited as the driving force of comprehension.

1.1 The Dual-Route Access to Meaning

The traditional view of language understanding relies on *compositionality*: The meaning of a sentence (or a discourse) is a function of the meaning of its constituents and the way they are syntactically combined (Partee, 1995). More precisely, the associated theoretical strategy sustained in the generative tradition (Chomsky, 1965; Pinker, 1999) is that syntax provides the primary mode of meaning combination in language: Syntactic rules do no more than determine which symbol sequence works as units for syntactic purposes, while meaning derives from the lexical conceptual structure. In other words, reading a sentence consists of linearly accessing the meaning of the words stored in the lexicon and then integrating them within the abstract hierarchical structure. This stance encourages a *bottom-up*, or building block, model of meaning where the interpretation mechanism is incremental: The meanings of the words are composed into syntactic units and aggregated until reaching a complete interpretation.

Nevertheless, there is extensive experimental evidence from psycholinguistic and neurolinguistic research against traditional compositionality (Baggio, 2021; Baggio, Van Lambalgen, & Hagoort, 2012; Ferreira, Bailey, & Ferraro, 2002; Ferreira & Patson, 2007; Mollica et al., 2020, among others). These findings can be synthesized into two fundamental observations (Baggio, 2018, p. 19):

- A comprehender generates interpretations based on the semantic relations between words, not necessarily encoded or reflected by the grammar, and
- A comprehender tends to generate semantic representations that could bypass or collide with syntactic analyses, resulting in superficial and even inaccurate interpretations.

These observations argue for a more *top-down* model, in which our semantic expectations drive comprehension: The linguistic elements function as cues to activate our extensive linguistic knowledge stored in the long-term memory. This knowledge encompasses various facets, such as the frequency of use of certain expressions, common associations, and event schemas. Consequently, linguistic knowledge transcends mere lexical components and transforms into the "cognitive organization of one's experience with language" (Bybee, 2006, p. 771). Moreover, experimental studies have revealed a consistent pattern: When the comprehender accesses information congruent with their preexisting or pre-activated knowledge, facilitation effects in processing occur (faster reading times, low N400, etc.). The linguistic theories rooted in these assumptions endorse a *noncompositional* mechanism of meaning interpretation. They advocate a model of language where linguistic knowledge comes from direct linguistic experience and sentence processing is constraint-based, probabilistic, and reliant on expectations.

Although the ongoing debate has opened the possibility that these two strategies (compositional and noncompositional access to meaning) are not mutually incompatible, few linguistic theories have thus far bothered to elucidate how the two mechanisms could be integrated within a unified framework of sentence processing. Notably, theories within the fields of psycholinguistics, theoretical linguistics, and computational linguistics have offered different perspectives on uncovering the cognitive systems behind language, describing their characteristics, and modeling them. On one end, experimental results from different research areas have shed light on the mechanisms that could underlie human language comprehension. However, our knowledge about the language system remains scattered: Psycholinguistic studies usually focus on language processing subtasks (e.g., lexical access) or modules (e.g., morphology, syntax) without being aggregated into a unified framework. Conversely, linguistic theories provide a rigorous formalism for language description, but they still have difficulty integrating the variability of language productions observed in behavioral experiments. To this day, it remains challenging to find in the existing literature a comprehensive model that unifies the different observations on language understanding into a unique architecture (Blache, 2017). However, there is a family of linguistic theories whose fundamental assumption could make it possible to integrate findings from multiple research fields.

1.2 A Constructionist View of Language

The behavioral evidence surrounding noncompositionality points to a model of linguistic representation that is in line with the assumptions of the usage-based models of language (Bybee, 2010; Croft, 1991, 2001; Langacker, 1987; Tomasello, 2009) and the Construction Grammar (CxG) paradigm (Hilpert, 2019; Hoffmann, 2022b; Hoffmann & Trousdale, 2013; Ungerer & Hartmann, 2023). CxG refers to a family of models based on the assumption that grammar is more than simply a formal system consisting of stable but arbitrary rules for defining well-formed sequences. Besides their specificities, all constructionist theories agree on a fundamental claim: Grammar consists of meaningful and symbolic form–meaning mappings, called *constructions* (Goldberg, 1995, 2006, 2019). The definition and operationalization of "construction" are still under debate, and each formalism proposes a slightly different criterion (see Ungerer & Hartmann, 2023 for a recent discussion on the definition of constructions). In the more general sense, constructions are processing units or chunks, from morphemes or words, to partially and fully lexicalized expressions, to schematic and productive patterns of language – such as Passive or Ditransitive constructions (Goldberg, 2003), up to even genres and text types (Hoffman & Bergs, 2018). For instance, the comparative correlative construction (Hoffmann, Brunner, & Horsch, 2020; also "Covariational Conditional"; cf. Culicover & Jackendoff, 1999) "The Xer, the Yer," such as

(2) *The more you know, the less you understand.*

has specific syntactic and semantic properties. First, both clauses are introduced by an element that "resembles" the English definite article *the*, which instead is followed by comparative phrases. Semantically, English speakers identify the cause–effect relationship between the two clauses, which is not marked at any syntactic level. Thus, both the syntax and the meaning of the construction are not entirely predictable by any abstract rule.

   At the same time, a syntactic pattern like the Double Object construction has a meaning independently of the words that compose the construction. People reading a sentence like

(3) *She mooped him something.*

interpret the made-up word *moop* as "to give" because the abstract pattern V Obj$_1$ Obj$_2$ communicates itself the concept of transfer between two persons (Goldberg, 2019, p. 29).

Constructions form a structured inventory of a speaker's knowledge of the conventions of their language, called the *constructicon* (Diessel, 2023): Each construction constitutes a node in the taxonomic network of constructions, and taxonomic relations allow us to distinguish different types of grammatical knowledge. However, there is no complete agreement about how such taxonomies emerge. Formal models such as Sign-Based CxG (Sag, 2012) assume that only "idiosyncratic morphological, syntactic, lexical, semantic, pragmatic or discourse-functional properties must be represented as an independent node in the constructional network in order to capture a speaker's knowledge of their language" (Croft & Cruse, 2004, p. 263). Conversely, usage-based approaches – that is, Radical CxG (Croft, 2001) or Cognitive CxG (Goldberg, 2003) – advocate that constructions can be of any linguistic pattern used enough to be memorized (or *entrenched*; cf. Blumenthal-Dramé, 2012) in the long-term memory (Goldberg, 2006). Specifically, the assumption is that linguistic units that are more frequently encountered become more accessible and are preferred. According to this thesis, the most entrenched linguistic units tend to shape the language system in terms of patterns of use, at the expense of less frequent and thus less well-entrenched words or phrases. This account opens to a more *redundant* view of the lexicon: Although we do not technically need to memorize the word form *cats* because, in principle, it can be formed with a productive rule *cat+s*, it could be memorized in the lexicon because we have encountered it thousands of times in everyday language (Hilpert, 2021, p. 21). The same observation could be done for phrases. For instance, *read a book* is a semantic transparent chunk; that is, we can identify the meanings of its parts and how they were combined to generate the final interpretation. Even though we could build the meaning of the expression "on the fly" using a compositional, incremental mechanism, this sequence was heard and used so many times to be stored as a whole; thus, interpretation becomes the act of retrieving the stored meaning. Using Goldberg's words, "memory is cheap. There is a good deal of evidence that we retain an enormous amount of information about the language(s) we witness" (Goldberg, 2019, p. 54).

However, that does not mean that people retain frequently observed word combinations as atomic units (as this would quickly result in a combinatorial explosion), but memory traces have an internal structure. Thus, representations of related memories overlap neurally, mitigating the concern about a combinatorial explosion (Goldberg, 2019). Moreover, the cognitive capacity of pattern detection and schematization (Bybee, 2010) allows the storage of more abstract construction from specific instances. Going back to the previous example, speakers redundantly store frequent plural forms in addition to a general plural construction, or an entire expression together with the abstract transitive pattern.

Placing constructions as the fundamental unit of language has the consequence of blurring the distinction between words of the lexicon and the rules of grammar. Contrary to generative theories, CxG argues that the architecture of the grammar is not layered in distinct modules, but different properties (morphological, prosodic, syntactic, semantic) together constitute the form that allows the construction to be identified, and when it is recognized, it is possible to access the associated meaning directly. This holistic view emphasizes the importance of surface structure, that is, the concrete utterances that a hearer is exposed to, as opposed to mainstream generative grammar, which primarily focuses on hidden syntactic processes not directly observable in the final output (Goldberg, 2013). As a joint representation of syntax and semantics, constructions provide a powerful mechanism for investigating many different linguistic phenomena (Diessel, 2019).

Despite the vast possibilities this framework offers for linguistic description and language modeling, some issues are still to be addressed. For instance, while we agree with the assumption that the lexicon is a repository of constructions, it is unclear which factors drive the memorization of specific chunks. The question about which constructions are stored in long-term memory and which aspects can be constructed online in working memory is yet to be fully answered and has consequences on the mechanisms governing sentence processing. In that regard, one more issue has to be figured out: What is the most appropriate and acceptable representation of constructional *meaning*? Toward a complete model of language comprehension, a further challenge is to give a semantic representation that could be coherent with the usage-based perspective and could account for the evidence that lexical knowledge is quite detailed, often idiosyncratic and verb specific, and often accessible at the earliest possible stage in sentence processing. Finally, while the majority of approaches have focused on grammatical description, only a few efforts have been carried on to operationalize CxG as computational modeling, with the exception of Fluid CxG (Steels, 2011) and Embodied CxG (Bergen & Chang, 2013).

To conclude, the core of this Element is investigating the relationship between constructions and compositionality, as the title of this work suggests. Indeed, constructionist approaches do not refute compositionally per se, but reformulate this paradigm in terms of the combination of constructions ("weak compositionality"; cf. Michel, 2023, p. 566):

> By recognizing the existence of contentful constructions we can save the compositionality in a weakened form: the meaning of an expression is the result of integrating the meaning of the lexical items into the meanings of constructions. (Goldberg, 1995, p. 16)

Consequently, the CxG framework turns out to be the best way to unify the different compositional and noncompositional mechanisms observed in language due to its key assumptions. Nevertheless, there is no consensus regarding the manner in which constructions interact with each other to license a specific utterance (Boas, 2021, p. 64). Overall, this Element is focused on reviewing the different insights about language processing, which aspects are already depicted in CxG, and which ones still need to be addressed by future research.

THEORETICAL CLAIMS OF CONSTRUCTION GRAMMAR
Adapted from Goldberg (2013, p. 15–16)

1. **Language as language use**. Our linguistic knowledge comes from linguistic experience: our lexicon and grammar are shaped by repeated exposure to specific utterances.
2. **Construction are the fundamental units of language**. Constructions are conventionalized associations of a form and a function, which apply not only to words but also to syntactic structures, thus guaranteeing a certain uniformity of representation of linguistic facts.
3. **The importance of the surface structure** Meaning is directly associated with surface structure, without derivations or transformations.
4. **The construct-i-con**. Grammar is a network of constructions, hierarchically organized through inheritance relations.
5. **There is a continuum from what is stored to what is processed**. There is no dichotomy between interpreting stored linguistic units and assembling expressions "on the fly"; there is just a *continuum* from stored items, highly predictable sequences, and completely compositional ones.
6. **Meaning emerges through context**. The meaning of a construction is inherently rooted in its contexts of use.

1.3 Compositionality, Productivity, Creativity

As introduced in the first paragraph of this Element, the surprising fact about language is that people can constantly generate (and understand) never-ever-produced utterances. Chomsky defined this property as the "creative aspect" of language: "[A]n essential property of language is that it provides the means for expressing indefinitely many thoughts and for reaching appropriately in an indefinite range of new situations" (Chomsky, 1965, p. 6). More recently, Adger affirmed:

> The fact that sentences hardly reoccur shows us that we use our language in an incredibly rich, flexible, and creative way . . . . Virtually every sentence we utter is novel. New to ourselves, and quite often new to humanity. We come up with phrases and sentences as we need to, and we make them express what we need to express. We do this with incredible ease. We don't think about it, we just do it. We create language throughout our lives, and respond creatively to the language of others. (Adger, 2019, p. 2)

Chomsky and the generative tradition thus seem to suggest that linguistic creativity is "combinatorial" and "productive" (Bergs, 2018, p. 278): It involves creating something entirely new using existing rules in almost infinite ways. The success of the principle of compositionality thus relies on its ability to explain the most attractive property of language: *creativity*. However, before introducing compositionality in the next section, it is essential to step back and understand how linguistic creativity is defined (especially in the realm of CxG). Let us start with some creative expressions:

(4)   a.   *She smiled him in the door* (Goldberg, 2019, p. 61).
      b.   *The mother of all battles* (Hartmann & Ungerer, 2023, p. 5).
      c.   *Messi is the Mozart of football* (Hoffmann, 2019, p. 5).
      d.   *Weapons of mass distraction* (Giora et al., 2004).

The following expressions are likely to be unfamiliar to most readers and, therefore, by the previous definition can be considered creative utterances. However, according to Sampson (2016), there are two distinct types of creativity: F-creativity (fixed creativity), which produces examples drawn from a predetermined and established inventory, and E-creativity (extending/enlarging creativity), which goes beyond the system rules. According to this dichotomy, many linguistic phenomena traditionally assumed as "creative" are, in fact, examples of F-creativity, as new sentences are the result of grammatical rules (Hoffmann, 2018).

The term *productivity* is used in linguistics to refer to the "original use of established possibilities of the language" (Leech, 2014, p. 24). For instance, syntactic productivity concerns "the range of lexical items that may fill the slots of constructions" (Perek, 2016, p. 66). In accordance with CxG's assumptions, one uses and extends preexisting constructions to generate novel utterances. This is exemplified in (4a), where the use of a typical intransitive verb (e.g., *smiled*) as transitive in a caused-motion construction forces a creative new meaning, such as "She caused him to move the door by smiling." Mismatches between the typical environments in which a verb is used and its occurrence in a new and creative way are widely discussed as *valency coercion* (Goldberg, 1995). Several studies in CxG have investigated this construction productivity, and in particular Goldberg (2019) offers an extensive review focusing on explaining "the partial productivity of grammatical constructions."

Even though many new expressions arise from productivity (of F-creativity), the question of "how do speakers use their grammar to create E-creative utterances" remains a topic of debate (Hoffmann, 2022a, p. 280). According to Bergs (2018), a source of E-creativity relies on the "intentional manipulation of linguistic structure" (p. 281), usually exemplified by linguistic *extravagance*, that is, to talk in such a way that you are noticed (Haspelmath, 1999; Ungerer & Hartmann, 2020). The use of formulaic patterns drawn from a fixed template, like in (4b) (namely, *snowclones*; cf. Hartmann & Ungerer, 2023) can be considered creative. They represent an interesting case because, even if they transmit a hyperbolic meaning fulfilling a specific pragmatic function, they still derive from a partially fixed construction. As such, these expressions illustrate the complex interplay between creativity and productivity (Ungerer & Hartmann, 2023).

Other examples of proper creative constructs are metaphorical expressions, like the one in (4c), which are governed by the general cognitive process of Conceptual Blending (Fauconnier & Turner, 2002; Turner, 2018). This mental operation constructs a partial match between two input mental spaces (FOOT-BALL and CLASSIC MUSIC, in this example) and selectively projects from those inputs into a novel "blended" mental space, resulting in a new meaning (Messi is a genius on the football pitch, just as Mozart was a musical genius; cf. Hoffmann, 2019). However, even apparently, rule-breaking phenomena like the production of a novel metaphor rely on established patterns (i.e., entrenched construction X-is-the-Y-of-Z; cf. Fauconnier & Turner, 2002) and on established mechanisms. As Bergs and Kompa (2020, p. 14) observes: "Still, even the most creative metaphor has to use established means (analogy) and comply with most of the rules governing language use and linguistic interaction. Thus, metaphors are actually also examples of F-creativity in the widest sense; they do not expand the rules of language as such."

Other research domains propose alternative models for linguistic creativity. One such theory is the Optimal Innovation hypothesis, which posits that the aesthetics of creative productions are best explained by variations of familiar material (Giora et al., 2004). According to this theory, specific minimal modifications of familiar expressions can be more pleasurable than entirely novel creations. For instance, the neologism in (4d) is optimally innovative because it induces a novel response while enabling the retrieval of a salient stimulus, the familiar expression "weapons of mass destruction." The question is: Are utterances of this type examples of F-creativity (as they relate to the familiar and use a specific mechanism) or of pure E-creativity?

Despite the considerable research on linguistic creativity, the examples above reveal that a consensus on what constitutes a creative expression has yet to be reached. As Maybin (2015, p. 34) stated: "While everyday language creativity is now an established area of ongoing linguistic research, there is a continuing lack of clear agreement about the precise definition and scope of creativity itself." Generally, the complex relation between productivity and creativity is far from being defined: Given that language is a complex system, it is challenging to define expressions entirely unconstrained by any rules ("All use of natural human language ultimately is F-creative"; cf. Bergs & Kompa, 2020, p. 18). In a broader sense, creativity can be viewed as a gradient phenomenon ranging from systematic productivity to extravagant stimuli that generalize from existing schemata. This Element focuses more on the F-creativity aspect of language, a "constrained" form of creativity (Goldberg, 2019), focusing on how the generation and comprehension of new expressions relate to the familiar and the mechanisms we can exploit to generate novel (but not necessarily creative) utterances apart from compositionality.

1.4 Roadmap

What is compositionality's role in today's models of language and sentence processing? How do we process both familiar and novel expressions? How can observations from experimental data be transposed into a formal theory of language representation and processing? This Element connects various linguistic theories and behavioral observations about processes governing semantic interpretation, arguing that CxG provides a more suitable linguistic formalism to explain language comprehension.

This Element is organized as follows. First, Section 2 introduces one of the two protagonists of the title: compositionality. Specifically, it discusses the notion of Fregean compositionality, traditionally believed to be the sole explanation for our ability to understand and create new sentences, and illustrates how this principle was used for describing the mechanism of meaning composition in traditional formalisms, constructionist approaches, and distributional models of meaning. Complementary, Section 3 examines studies in psycholinguistics and neurolinguistics that challenge this traditional view. The behavioral outcomes suggest a model of linguistic representation consistent with usage-based constructionist approaches, blurring the distinction between stored and nonstored sequences and productive and nonproductive patterns. Furthermore, Section 4 introduces the main claim of this Element: Systematic processes of language productivity are mainly explainable by analogical inferences rather than sequential compositional operations. Novel expressions are produced and understood "on the fly" by analogy with familiar ones. The section delves into the characteristics of analogical reasoning and explores the nature of linguistic analogy to support the proposal that analogical processing forms the basis of the human capability to generate new utterances. Finally, Section 5 proposes a redefinition of the role of compositionality as a property of natural language and as the only mechanism in sentence comprehension, suggesting that compositionality is only one of the possible explanations for the human ability to comprehend and produce an endless number of novel utterances.

In the end, readers will realize the complexity of rethinking a linguistic theory that formalizes the coexistence of different mechanisms to interpret any expression, from the most common to the never-encountered-before ones.

2 The Problem of Compositionality as a Processing Principle

One common remark about human thought and language is their outstanding expressive power to assemble meaningful parts into endlessly novel configurations. As observed in everyday language, we have a potentially open-ended capacity to produce and understand novel meaningful sentences we have never heard before. For instance, let us consider the following sentence.

(5) *Purple cats are fluffy.*

Any English speaker could understand this sentence, even if it sounds odd and plausibly it was never encountered before: This is because comprehenders know the meanings of *purple*, *cats*, and *fluffy* and how to construct the meaning of a novel sentence from the meanings of its parts. By combining morphemes into words, words into phrases, and phrases into sentences, natural language is exceptionally productive and expressive.

If it is possible to easily comprehend the meaning of a new sentence, there must be a systematic procedure for determining that meaning. Crucially, a fundamental question that any theory of language should address is: *How do people glean meaning from language?* (Goldberg, 2015). In other words, it should propose a hypothesis about the mechanism that enables the construction of meaning from smaller units of meaning. Classical theories posit the existence of a compositionality principle, which stipulates that the meaning of a complex expression is a function of the meanings of its parts. The following pages summarize what the Principle of Compositionality is, the primary arguments supporting it, and its formalization within linguistic theory.

2.1 The Principle of Compositionality: Definitions and Main Assumptions

The traditional presumption in philosophy and linguistics is that language and thought are *compositional* (Martin & Baggio, 2020): The meaning of a complex expression is entirely determined by its structure and the meanings of its constituents – once we specify what the parts mean and how they are put together, there is no more leeway regarding the meaning of the whole. This view is referred to as the *Principle of Compositionality*, also called Frege's Principle by the name of Gottlob Frege, credited with having first formulated this notion – although there are problems with this attribution (Pelletier, 1994, p. 24). The principle of compositionality was first introduced as a constraint on the relation between the syntax and the semantics of languages, and it was later postulated as an adequacy condition for other representational systems such as structures of mental concepts (Hinzen, Werning, & Machery, 2012a).

Broadly, the principle of compositionality is typically defined as follows:

> The meaning of a whole is a function of the meanings of the parts and of the way they are syntactically combined. (Partee, 1995, p. 312)

> The meaning of a complex expression is determined by the meanings of its constituents and by its structure. (Szabó, 2000, p. 1)

These definitions are just two of the most cited, although several variants have been formulated (Hinzen, Werning, & Machery, 2012b). The common aspect of both versions is that the notions of content and structure are admittedly vague: The nature of the principle can be made precise only with an explicit theory of meaning and syntax, together with a full specification of what is required by the relation "is a function of" (Pelletier, 2016). In this sense, compositionality is highly theory-dependent (Partee, 2004, p. 154).

Linguistic theories adopting the compositional hypothesis diverge on several points depending on the theoretical assumptions regarding the representation of words' meanings (i.e., the building blocks of the sentence), the syntactic rules governing sentence structure, and the processes implicated in meaning construction. Among others, they diverge on whether syntactic analysis recedes and supplies its output prior to semantic analysis, or whether syntactic and semantic analyses are combined (as exemplified in the Head-driven Phrase Structure Grammar, or HPSG; Sag & Pollard, 1994), with syntactic rules

integrating the semantic information obtained from the elements they combine. Additionally, these theories differ in the form of the semantic output:
a logical formula in first-order logic, a lambda expression, or a typed-feature
representation, inter alia.

Although several variants of the principle have been formulated, the core
idea is that the principle of compositionality advocates for a bottom-up, or
building block model of meaning: The meaning of the whole expression is
incrementally built from the meanings of its constituent parts (Goldberg, 2015).
The principle also entails a *modular* vision of the interpretation process; that is,
there is a clear separation between syntax and semantics. This so-called division
of labor works in most formal approaches in the following way: Lexical semantics represents the meanings of words, and syntax governs the combination of
words into larger units of meaning and ascribes the relationships between words
within these larger units.

Furthermore, the principle presupposes the concepts of localism and incrementality. In the first place, *localism* pertains to whether compositional operations are local or global in nature. As outlined by Pagin and Westerståhl
(2010a), the meaning of a complex term can be derived from (1) the meaning of its immediate "children" within the syntactic structure (considered in a
tree-like fashion) regardless of the process by which their meaning was built
up (strong compositionality), or (2) from its total (global) structure and the
meanings of its constituent atomic parts (weak compositionality). In the latter interpretation, complex terms may exhibit different meanings depending
on the larger expression of which they are part. Hupkes et al. (2020) exemplified the problem in arithmetic terms: The outcome of 14 − (2 + 3) does
not change when the subsequence (2 + 3) is replaced by 5, a sequence with
the same (local) meaning, but a different structure (strong version). However,
the strong hypothesis is controversial in natural language, especially in the case
of disambiguation of a phrase or word in context. Conversely, *incrementality*
assumes that the interpretation process follows rigidly the same order in which
the constituents are combined to form complex expressions, step by step, in
a deterministic fashion. At each step, the interpretative operation builds the
semantic value of the current node and makes it available for further steps.
Importantly, once a semantic value has been ascribed to a particular utterance,
it cannot be changed. These two properties introduce a perspective on meaning composition that presents certain challenges. First, localism yields that the
assignment of a semantic value to a node must not rely on external factors
beyond the current segment of the sentence under analysis. Second, incrementality asserts that once a semantic representation has been assigned, the meaning
remains unchanged, regardless of any subsequent constituents, whether they be

phrases, sentences, or discourse (Gayral, Kayser, & Lévy, 2005). Nonetheless, as will be argued in the subsequent section, the context of use assumes a pivotal role in human interpretation, challenging a strong and incremental view of compositionality.

The principle of compositionality has been compelling for many reasons, even if it has been widely criticized (in fact, approximately 318 arguments against it can be found in the literature, cf. Pelletier, 1994). Without delving into specific details, the following section sketches the traditional arguments favoring compositionality together with their main criticisms (cf. Pagin & Westerståhl, 2010b for a comprehensive review of arguments both in favor of and in opposition to compositionality).

2.1.1 *The Arguments of Compositionality*

The standard arguments in favor of the principle originate from supposed "facts" about language and are used as justifications for the necessity of compositionality (Baggio, 2021, p. 4). In the following boxtext we report the main arguments, as summarized by Goldberg (2015).

STANDARD ARGUMENTS IN FAVOR OF COMPOSITIONALITY
Derived from Goldberg (2015) and influenced by Dowty (2007, p. 3–4).

a. Speakers produce and listeners parse sentences that they have never spoken nor heard before.
b. Speakers and listeners generally agree upon the meanings of sentences.
c. Since there exists an infinite number of sentences, they cannot all be memorized.
d. There must be some procedure for determining meaning.
e. Sentences are generated by some grammar of the language.
f. The procedure for interpreting sentences must be determined, in some way or the other, by the syntactic structures generated by the grammar together with the words.

The first and most familiar argument in favor of compositionality is that it can explain our ability to produce and understand sentences we have never heard before (*productivity*, cf. points a., c., and d. in the box). The argument goes as follows. Since speakers are able to understand a sentence S they have never encountered, it must be that they know something on the basis of which they can figure out, without any additional information, what S means. What can this knowledge be? The only thing that could plausibly be is knowledge of the syntactic structure of S and of the individual meanings of the simple constituents of *S*. However, this argument has been criticized on the ground of several considerations. Szabó (2012) questioned the argument of productivity, observing it assumes "that we already understand expressions we have never heard before. What is the evidence for this? The fact that when we hear them we understand them shows nothing more than the information necessary to determine what they mean is available to us immediately after they have been uttered." Reformulating, what is evidence for the claim that we already understand certain expressions we have never heard before? Is it true that we always rely on syntax in interpreting novel expressions?

A related argument in favor of compositionality (points e. and f. in the box) is the concept of *systematicity*, a term introduced by Fodor and Pylyshyn to denote that "[t]he ability to produce/understand some sentences is *intrinsically* connected to the ability to produce/understand certain others" (Fodor & Pylyshyn, 1988, p. 37). In the simplest manifestation, if speakers comprehend a sentence of the form *t*R*u*, such as *John loves Mary*, they are expected to similarly comprehend the corresponding sentence *u*R*t* (e.g., *Mary loves John*). Nonetheless, this intuitive property becomes relatively weak once we start considering more complex cases. For instance, not every word substitution within an expression remains meaningful. For example, given the phrases *within an hour* and *without a watch*, it is challenging to derive meaningful interpretations for *within a watch* and *without an hour* (Baggio, Van Lambalgen, & Hagoort, 2012, p. 657). Moreover, the mere comprehension of *red car* and *tall building* does not necessarily imply the comprehension of *red building* and *tall car* (Szabó, 2012).

In this sense, the argument of systematicity delves into the very nature of natural language: Are sentences resulting from grammatical recombination inherently meaningful or not? It is debatable to what extent this really holds, and sentences like Chomsky's *Colorless green ideas sleep furiously* (Chomsky, 1957) have been used to argue that not all grammatical sentences are meaningful. Nevertheless, even if we were to assume that all grammatical sentences are meaningful, this alone does not establish the necessity of compositionality or any form of systematic semantics for its explanation (Pagin & Westerståhl, 2010b, p. 5).

Finally, while systematicity can be empirically observed to a certain extent, productivity remains a more contentious issue. It is, indeed, impossible to conclusively demonstrate the existence of an infinite number of complex expressions in natural languages (Pullum & Scholz, 2010). Even if human memory were theoretically capable of generating infinitely long sentences, the finite lifespan of individuals would preclude such a possibility. Consequently, the argument about the productivity of language is generally regarded as more contentious than that of systematicity (Hupkes et al., 2020), although it is the most intuitive one.

Another point, referred to as the *methodological argument* (Baggio, Van Lambalgen, & Hagoort, 2012), posits that compositionality serves as a necessary constraint in semantic analysis. The principle of compositionality provides an operationalized way to compute the meaning of complex linguistic expressions. It represents indeed one of the most straightforward explanations: Starting from the meanings of its atomic constituents and following its syntactic structure, the interpretation of a complex expression unfolds progressively, step by step, from the atomic components to the most elaborate ones. Despite its widespread appeal, this argument, too, falls short of validating compositionality. The ability of compositional semantic theories to account for certain phenomena does not inherently imply that these theories are effective because they are compositional; in other words, it does not prove that compositionality is a property of natural language.

These concerns, though merely a fraction of the broader issues at hand, have initiated an extensive investigation aimed at establishing the limits and refining the concept of compositionality through empirical data and cognitive insights. The subsequent section delves into the formalization of compositionality in both traditional linguistic frameworks and more recent computational methodologies.

2.2 Modeling Compositionality

2.2.1 Compositionality in Formal Semantics

The principle of compositionality stands as a foundational claim in *Formal Semantics*, a well-established approach in linguistic theory (Groenendijk & Stokhof, 2005; Partee, 2016; Partee, ter Meulen, & Wall, 1990). Formal Semantics encompasses a range of semantic theories, all employing standard methodologies grounded in symbolic logic, mathematics, and mathematical logic to rigorously formulate well-defined theories concerning the semantics of natural languages (King, 2006).

The philosopher and logician Richard Montague (e.g., 1970b; 1973) was one of the first to argue that the relation between syntax and semantics in natural language could be regarded as not essentially different from the relation between syntax and semantics in a formal language, such as the language of first-order logic. He articulated this idea in the following words:

> There is in my opinion no important theoretical difference between natural languages and the artificial languages of logicians; indeed, I consider it possible to comprehend the syntax and semantics of both kinds of languages

within a single natural and mathematically precise theory. On this point I differ from a number of philosophers, but agree, I believe, with Chomsky and his associates. (Montague, 1970b)

Accordingly, natural language could be "translated" into the metalanguage of logic, as, for instance, the language of predicate calculus. Within the Montague Grammar tradition, the principle of compositionality assumes a pivotal role in articulating the relation of semantics to syntax. It states that the semantic interpretation for a language is defined as some *homomorphism* (a structure-preserving mapping) from syntax to semantics (a gentle introduction to this concept is provided by Janssen and Partee 1997, p. 448–450). In other words, the syntactic operations that combine syntactic expressions must match the meaning operations, forming complex meanings from simpler ones. Goldberg (1995, p. 13) illustrates this claim as follows:

$$\sigma(x +_{syn-comp} y) = \sigma(x) +_{sem-comp} \sigma(y), \tag{1}$$

where σ is a function from syntax to semantics, $+_{syn-comp}$ is a rule of syntactic composition, and $+_{sem-comp}$ is a rule of semantic composition. The formula formally conveys that the interpretation of the entire expression results from applying the meanings of the immediate constituents (and only by those meanings) via a semantic operation that aligns directly with the corresponding syntactic operation. It is worth noticing that having a compositional interpretation structured in this manner represents a straightforward way of ensuring that each of the infinitely potential syntactic structures within a language will receive a clearly defined interpretation (Groenendijk & Stokhof, 2005).

The perspective and the technical apparatus Montague offered have significantly impacted the study of natural language semantics, paving the way for a wide range of Formal Semantic approaches, from model-theoretic to proof-theoretic semantics. Besides their specificities, any compositional formal semantic framework provides

1. a knowledge or a semantic representation of linguistic expressions in a logic,
2. some mechanisms for combining them in the form of formal rules.

Classically, semantic information is depicted in terms of feature-value structures, and logic is used both as a description language and calculus for constructing the meaning. In these approaches, the meaning is assembled starting from atomic objects (typically the meaning of words) and incrementally combined into larger structures. This mechanism constitutes the basis of compositionality. It is noticeable that this formalization requires an explicit representation of both types of information: the information associated with the constituents (typically lexical semantics) and the meaning composition mechanisms. The standard approach is to use first-order logic and model meaning composition as function application (Montague, 1970a; Partee, ter Meulen, & Wall, 1990). The semantic representation of the phrase *Alex smiled* can be expressed as in Equation 2. In this representation, the proper noun "Alex" is denoted by a constant (a), while the predicate "smiled" is expressed as a lambda term, signifying a function that can be applied to arguments of the appropriate type. The application of "smiled" function to the argument "Alex" (as illustrated in the third row) results in the final expression, where the bound variable (x), found within the lambda term, is replaced with the argument expression a (the example is adapted from Martin & Baggio, 2020).

$$\begin{aligned} &\text{Alex: } a \\ &\text{smiled: } \lambda x.smile(x) \\ &\text{Alex smiled: } [\lambda x.smile(x)](a) \\ &\longrightarrow smile(a) \end{aligned} \tag{2}$$

In lambda calculus, the process of function application allows the identification of the arguments and the predicates to be gathered into formulae, thanks to a mapping function from syntax to semantics. The integration of quantifiers and modalities completes the logical model, employing specific mechanisms based on more intricate calculi. This mechanism, which remains relatively consistent across various theories, relies on two foundational premises: first, that meaning can be dissected into fundamental, atomic components; and second, that a linear and incremental mechanism exists for assembling these components into abstract structures.

This approach constitutes the basis of numerous semantic formal frameworks, particularly those focused on the interface between syntax, semantics, and discourse. Noteworthy examples include Discourse Representation Theory (Kamp & Reyle, 1993) and Combinatory Categorial Grammar (Steedman, 2001). From a computational perspective as well, the Montagovian perspective of compositionality has long been a cornerstone in natural language understanding approaches. Extensive work has been carried out in this direction within the logic programming paradigm (Colmerauer, 1982; Shieber & Pereira, 1987), and more recently, within the theoretical framework of Categorial Grammars (Bos et al., 2004; Moot, 2012). Additionally, a more recent framework exploring semantic representation with minimal structures has been proposed in the Head-Driven Phrase Structure Grammar paradigm, known as *Minimal Recursion Semantics* (Copestake et al., 2005). This framework introduces key notions, such as under-specification and a generalization of the interface between semantics and other domains.

However, the traditional formal analysis of meaning composition is acknowledged to exhibit certain limitations in terms of its power and expressive capacity. On the representation side, it is unclear how lambda terms precisely capture the intricate nuances of the meanings of constituent expressions. Formal approaches struggle to encapsulate content words in all their richness – and, by extension, the array of inferences drawn from lexical information (Boleda & Herbelot, 2016). For instance, while *man* and *dude* would have the same ontological representation (they both refer to male humans), they are not equivalent, as they have different connotations (Boleda & Herbelot, 2016). Different formalisms have been explored for modeling lexical meaning, employing richer data structures than lambda terms, with significant implications for theories concerning the process of semantic composition. On the composition side, a critical question emerges: whether meaning arises solely from the process of function application or from the interpretation of formulas within predicate logic. This dilemma becomes particularly pronounced when composition and interpretation do not mirror each other, giving rise to scenarios where a strong version of compositionality falls short of delivering comprehensive explanations (Martin & Baggio, 2020). Furthermore, it is essential to acknowledge that Formal Semantics does not encode the full spectrum of human linguistic experiences. Notably, analogical reasoning, a fundamental facet of human predictive cognition, lies beyond the scope of Formal Semantics (Boleda & Herbelot, 2016). Additionally, this formalism encounters difficulties in adequately describing numerous linguistic phenomena, including but not limited to co-compositionality (Pustejovsky, 2012) and coercion.

2.2.2 Compositionality in Generative Linguistics

The principle of compositionality has been a central assumption even within mainstream generative grammar. Jackendoff (1997, p. 48) asserted that these theories had been founded under a standard (and usually unspoken) hypothesis, which he designated as "syntactically transparent semantic composition" or *Simple Composition*. This concept corresponds to what Culicover and Jackendoff (2006) name Fregean compositionality and is grounded on the following assumptions:

1. All elements of content in the meaning of a sentence are found in the lexical conceptual structures (LCSs) of the lexical items composing the sentence.

2. The way the LCSs are combined is a function only of the way the lexical items are combined in syntactic structure (including argument structure). In particular,

- the internal structure of individual LCSs plays no role in determining how the LCSs are combined;
- pragmatics plays no role in determining how LCSs are combined.

Given this definition, Simple composition is governed entirely by syntactic structure, and lexical items are predominantly considered as semantically unde-composable entities, excluding any interaction between their internal structure and phrasal composition. Nevertheless, predicates of various categories are sometimes understood as having implicitly on some level more arguments than appear on the surface, that is, there are cases in which certain aspects of meaning do not seem to be represented in both its word components or its syntactic structure.

Consider, for instance, the following sentence:

(3) *The journalist begar the article after his coffee break.*

While it may not explicitly mention what the journalist began to do, it is unlikely that English speakers would find this sentence difficult to understand, and even most would interpret it as "The journalist began to write the article after his coffee break." This example is a classic case of *logical metonymy* (Pustejovsky, 1995). Specifically, this phenomenon arises from a type clash between an event-selecting metonymic verb (e.g., *begin*) and an entity-denoting direct object (e.g., *article*), triggering the retrieval of a covert event (e.g., the act of writing). This phenomenon poses a challenge for traditional theories of compositionality (Asher, 2015) since it is the counterproof that interpretation cannot always be solely determined by syntactic structure. This raises the question of how the covert event is accessed and which cognitive processes are involved in its retrieval.

Another case in which simple compositionality fails is the *beneficiary dative construction*. In a double object construction such as

(4) *Bill baked Andy a cake,*

the indirect object *Andy* is understood as coming into possession of the direct object (*a cake*). However, the "possession" component of meaning does not reside in the meaning of any lexical words, but in the construction itself. A Fregean compositionality requires an explicit (but hidden) representation of possession in the syntactic structure.

The same observation can be formulated for the *sound–motion construction*, a linguistic phenomenon that links auditory or sound-related elements with motion or movement-related concepts in language and thought (Goldberg & Jackendoff, 2004; Levin & Hovav, 1995). This construction is often used to express or convey the idea that a particular sound or noise is associated with a particular type of motion, movement, or action. Here are some example sentences that illustrate this concept:

(5) a. *The water <u>gurgled</u> down the stream.*
   b. *The door <u>creaked</u> open.*

The sentences' meaning can be approximated to "The sound 'gurgled' is linked to the motion of water flowed down the stream, producing a gurgling sound," and "The door opened, creating a creaking sound." However, it is important to note that both "gurgle" and "creak" are verbs describing the emission of a sound, not verbs used to express motion. Consequently, within the sentences, there is no word that conveys the intended sense of the motion (Culicover & Jackendoff, 2006). The Simple Composition paradigm could not deal with these expressions because a hidden verb, such as "go," should be required in the syntax to fully capture the intended meaning.

The analysis of such cases raises both descriptive and theoretical problems that bear on the compositionality thesis, and they have led to a reformulation of a new hypothesis about meaning composition, that is, *Enriched Composition* (Jackendoff, 1997, p. 49):

1. The conceptual structure of a sentence may contain, in addition to the conceptual content of its LCSs, other material that is not expressed lexically, but that must be present in conceptual structure either (i) in order to achieve well-formedness in the composition of the LCSs into conceptual structure (coercion, to use Pustejovsky's term) or (ii) in order to satisfy the pragmatics of the discourse or extralinguistic context.
2. The way the LCSs are combined into conceptual structure is determined in part by the syntactic arrangement of the lexical items and in part by the internal structure of the LCSs themselves (Pustejovsky's cocomposition).

This reformulation of compositionality (Jackendoff, 1997; Pustejovsky, 1995) introduces complex lexical entries: Entities are associated with a complex structure (e.g., Pustejovsky's *qualia* structure) in the mental lexicon. Given this perspective, this linguistic phenomena can find a new reformulation. For the logical metonymy, for example, the covert event "must be present in [the] conceptual structure" (Jackendoff, 1997, p. 49). The introduction of this novel formalism carries profound implications: When lexical meanings are rich and internally developed data structures, the process of meaning composition becomes intricate and potentially defies straightforward description through function application. This realization gives rise to fundamental questions regarding the characteristics and extent of composition, including whether it involves a simple or complex function, involves single or multiple operations, functions independently or relies entirely on syntax, and more (Martin & Baggio, 2020).

2.2.3 Compositionality in Constructionist Approaches

It is frequently contended that constructional approaches either lack compositionality or explicitly deny semantic composition (Kay & Michaelis, 2012). However, compositional operations and a construction-based formalism to syntax are not inherently contradictory, and some constructionist approaches have been developed to formally integrate them into a unique representation. *Sign-Based Construction Grammar* (SBCG) (Michaelis, 2013; Sag, 2012; Sag, Boas, & Kay, 2012) has been the one more extensively focused on formally explaining syntactic and semantic composition through construction representation (Michaelis, 2015). Sign-Based Construction Grammar proposes a highly structured and taxonomically organized lexicon, based on two fundamental units, namely *signs* and *constructions*. Signs are feature structures that specify both syntactic and semantic properties and are formally represented as attribute-value matrices (AVMs; cf. Figure 1). This representation regards each expression of a language as a sign, as *words*, *lexemes*, and even *phrases* (Michaelis, 2015). Conversely, constructions are described as the means to derive more complex sign descriptions from simpler ones. Specifically, they are type constraints that specify (i) the properties that define a class of constructs (i.e., feature structures equivalent to local trees with signs at the nodes)

$$\begin{bmatrix} \textit{lexeme} \\[4pt] \text{FORM } \left\langle \textit{drink} \right\rangle \\[6pt] \text{SYN} \mid \text{VAL } \left\langle \text{NP} \begin{bmatrix} \text{overt} \\ \text{INST} \quad x \end{bmatrix}, \text{ NP} \begin{bmatrix} \text{(ini)} \\ \text{INST} \quad i \end{bmatrix} \right\rangle \\[10pt] \text{SEM} \mid \text{FRAMES } \left\langle \begin{bmatrix} \textit{drink-fr} \\ \text{DRINKER} \quad i \\ \text{DRAFT} \quad x \end{bmatrix}; \begin{bmatrix} \textit{animate-fr} \\ \text{INST} \quad i \end{bmatrix}; \begin{bmatrix} \textit{liquid-fr} \\ \text{INST} \quad x \end{bmatrix} \right\rangle \end{bmatrix}$$

Figure 1 A sign in SBCG (from Michaelis, 2015, p. 152). The lexeme *drink* is represented by syntactic (SYN) and semantic (SEM) constraints.

$$
subjpred\text{-}cxt \Rightarrow
\begin{bmatrix}
phrase \\
\text{MTR } [\text{ SYN } [\text{ VAL } \langle\rangle]] \\
\text{DTRS } < \text{X;H} > \\
\text{HD-DTR H}
\begin{bmatrix}
\text{SYN } \left[\text{CAT } \left[\text{VF } fin\right]\right] \\
\text{VAL } <\text{X}>
\end{bmatrix}
\end{bmatrix}
$$

Figure 2 A construction in SBCG (from Michaelis, 2015, p. 153). The *subject–predicate cxn* describes the mother sign of a basic clause. It contains a mother (MTR) feature with an empty valence list, a daughters (DTRS) feature with two items on its valence list, and a head daughter (H) that is a finite verb and has one item on its valence list (X, i.e., the subject of the clause).

and (ii) the way to construct a mother sign from one or more daughter signs (Michaelis, 2013). Constructions are descriptions of either classes of constructs (combinatoric constructions) or of lexemes (lexical class constructions). An example of the subject–predicate construction is provided in Figure 2.

Sign-Based Construction Grammar offers a robust formalism to construction-based syntax by relying on the mechanism of *unification*. This operation involves matching and merging the corresponding features from each linguistic structure (signs), ensuring that the resulting representation captures the combined form and meaning of the components. These constraints ensure that the unified feature structure is well-formed and conforms to the grammatical and semantic constraints of the language. Constraints may include syntactic rules, semantic roles, selectional restrictions, and other linguistic principles (Sag, 2012). For example, the feature structure of the construct subject–predicate is unified with those of the sign of the lexemes for the verb and the subject to create a representation of the entire fragment. Such a combination is possible because there is no conflicting attribute-value information between the two constructions (i.e., the AVMs are "unifiable"; cf. Chaves, 2019).

Therefore, while traditional syntactic approaches affirm that the interpretation of an expression is licensed by (i) a rule of syntactic composition and (ii) a rule of semantic composition (Equation (1)), SBCG proposes a unique linguistic object (a construction) that serves a similar function (Michaelis, in press). Overall, SBCG offers a formalism for construction-based syntax that is declarative and constraint-based (Michaelis, 2013).

This approach has the advantage of incorporating the CxG organization into a formalized framework. Specifically, it provides a means to explicitly specify the relationships between the various components of a construction. However, criticism has been leveled against SBCG, suggesting a tendency to prioritize formal-syntactic aspects over semantic considerations. For instance,

Sag (2010) proposes a comprehensive construction for filler-gap phenomena that completely lacks semantic content (defective constructions). This contrasts with a shared constructionist view (Goldberg, 2006; Hilpert, 2019) for which each construction, even the more abstract one, has associated a specific meaning (Ungerer & Hartmann, 2023).

Moreover, SBCG is a process-neutral approach that makes no predictions about the actual online parsing or production of constructions (Hoffmann, 2017). By contrast, there are two constructionist frameworks based on the unification of AVMs developed for the computational implementation of sentence processing, namely, Fluid Construction Grammar (FCG; Steels, 2013, 2017) and Embodied Construction Grammar (ECG; Bergen & Chang, 2005, 2013). Besides their formalisms, both are specifically developed for computational implementation (Hoffmann & Trousdale, 2013; Ungerer & Hartmann, 2023). In particular, FCG utilizes truth-conditional first-order predicate calculus, whereas ECG relies on mental simulation models and embodied schemas. Additionally, while FCG formalism accepts defective constructions, ECG constructions are always form-meaning pairings, though it does not deny the existence of purely form or meaning schemas (Hoffmann, 2017).

2.3 Distributional Approaches to Compositionality

Formal approaches assume that the meaning of words (constants that replace symbols into logical formulas) is one and just one, determined a priori, that is to say, "a lexical item must make approximately the same semantic contribution to each expression in which it occurs" (Fodor & Pylyshyn, 1988, p. 42). However, this assumption contrasts with the evidence that lexical meanings are context-sensitive, that is, they can "adapt" their meaning to fit a specific context and communicative situation, and generally, their use in contexts defines their semantic representation. That is to say, the distribution of the words constitutes one of the essential sources of information for accessing their meaning.

In this respect, *Distributional Semantics* (Boleda, 2020; Lenci, 2018; Lenci & Sahlgren, 2023) have provided a solid alternative framework for denoting word meaning in the past decades. Posing a radically different stance, Distributional Semantics aims at representing the word meaning as the contexts in which it occurs, rising from the so-called *Distributional Hypothesis* of lexical meaning (Firth, 1957; Harris, 1954; Sahlgren, 2008). Concretely, a Distributional Semantic Model represents the lexicon in terms of a vector space, where a lexical target is described as a numeric vector (also known as *embedding*) built by identifying its syntactic and lexical contexts in a corpus (Lenci, 2018). This computational implementation makes it possible to quantify the similarity between words using algebraic formulas while allowing room for semantic changes (Perek, 2016) and meaning shifts (Busso, Pannitto, & Lenci, 2018). Compared to formal representation, this approach has some advantages: (1) It provides a continuous representation that can easily tackle language's gradience and fuzziness; (2) it does not assume a priori semantic primitives, that is, it is not stipulative; and (3) representations are also explainable in terms of how we can cognitively build these (it is plausible with respect to learnability, cf. Miller & Charles, 1991).

Initial distributional approaches have been designed to represent word meaning by assigning each word to a single vector, produced as an abstraction over all its contexts of use. The logical next step involved understanding how to combine these representations to obtain vectors for phrases, sentences, and even larger pieces of text. Research in the last decade led, first and foremost, to methods integrating DSMs with formal symbolic theories of language: Semantic composition depends on an algebraic function that combines words, which are no longer described as symbolic representations but as distributional ones.

The approaches partaking this stance fall under the name of *Compositional Distributional Semantics Models* (CDSMs) (Baroni, Bernardi, & Zamparelli, 2014; J. Mitchell et al., 2010) and aim to explicitly apply the principle of compositionality to compute distributional vectors for phrases. Compositional Distributional Semantics Models produce representations of phrases by composing distributional vectors of words comprised in these phrases. As in classic Distributional Semantics for words, these models generate similar vectors for semantically similar sentences, regardless of length or structure. For example, *require attention* and *need treatment* should have a similar distributional signature, and they should be dissimilar to, that is, *attend a conference*.

Various strategies to compose word embeddings have been suggested (cf. Table 1). In the most influential papers on the topic, J. Mitchell and Lapata (2008, 2010) introduced several arithmetic operations for vector composition, operationalized as additive and multiplicative functions. For instance, the expression *fluffy cat* can be represented as

$$\overrightarrow{fluffy} + \overrightarrow{cat} = \overrightarrow{fluffy\ cat}, \tag{3}$$

in which the meaning of the phrase is a new embedding derived from the addition of word vectors. Compositional Distributional Semantics Models are usually evaluated on a phrase similarity task: For pairs of phrases, the similarity between their respective combined vectors is computed and these scores are compared with similarity ratings elicited from English speakers.

Table 1 Vector composition functions

Model	Function
Weighted additive	$\alpha\overrightarrow{fluffy} + \beta\overrightarrow{cat}$
Multiplicative	$\overrightarrow{fluffy} \odot \overrightarrow{cat}$
Full additive	$\mathbf{X}\overrightarrow{fluffy} + \mathbf{Y}\overrightarrow{cat}$
Lexical Function	$\mathbf{A}_{\text{fluffy}}\overrightarrow{cat}$
Fullex	$tanh([W_1, W_2]\begin{bmatrix} A_{\text{fluffy}} & \overrightarrow{cat} \\ A_{\text{cat}} & \overrightarrow{fluffy} \end{bmatrix}$

Note: $\odot$ stands for pointwise multiplication. α and β are scalar parameters, matrices $\mathbf{X}$ and $\mathbf{Y}$ represent syntactic relation slots (e.g., Adjective and Noun), matrix $\mathbf{A}$ represents a functional word (e.g., the adjective in an adjective–noun construction).
Source: References to the models, in order: J. Mitchell and Lapata (2008); J. Mitchell and Lapata (2008); Zanzotto et al. (2010); Baroni and Zamparelli (2010); Socher et al. (2013)

More complex models characterize composition by representing lexemes and phrases with matrices and tensors rather than with vectors alone (Socher et al., 2013; Zanzotto et al., 2010). For instance, the *Lexical Function model* denotes predicates (verbs and adjectives specifically) as functions mapping one noun meaning to another, coherently with the Montagovian view. Concretely, predicates are matrices, their nominal arguments are represented as vectors, and their multiplication results in the phrase vector (Baroni & Zamparelli, 2010). The Lexical Function model was one of the first attempts to represent formal semantic operations with DSMs and turned out to be very influential in the research area. However, the main limitation of this approach is the difficulty in scaling up to multi-argument sentences. Estimating the matrices and tensors for complex functional types such as transitive verbs can be very complex and may encounter data-sparseness problems. Paperno, Pham, and Baroni (2014) proposed a practical approximation of the Lexical Function model to address these limits, but it is hardly competitive with the much simpler additive models (Rimell et al., 2016).

Some authors also exploited neural networks to learn composition functions explicitly. An example is the recursive neural network (RNN) of Socher, Manning, and Ng (2010), in which representations for larger chunks are computed recursively obeying a predefined syntactic parse tree of the sentence. Specifically, the neural network induces a score for each pair of neighboring words, which measures how likely these two words are to be combined into a phrase, and simultaneously, it collapses the two words into an *n*-dimensional representation of the resulting phrase. This new phrase embedding replaces the words in the sequence and possibly becomes a child of another phrase spanning more words. This bottom-up process continues until the whole input sentence is mapped to the embedding space. An alternative approach proposed by Socher et al. (2012) was the matrix-vector RNN, which consists in representing each word by a vector and a matrix encoding its interaction with the syntactic sisters. Compositional representations for phrases and sentences are learned by a RNN in a supervised setting.

Finally, an alternative approach to compositional DSMs assumes that the representation of a sentence is not a vector but rather a logical form containing distributional vectors of the content words (Asher et al., 2016; Beltagy et al., 2016; Coecke, Sadrzadeh, & Clark, 2010; Garrette, Erk, & Mooney, 2014).

Among all compositional functions proposed here, vector addition still shows remarkable performances on various tasks, such as phrase similarity or paraphrase detection (Asher et al., 2016; Rimell et al., 2016), outperforming more complex methods, such as the Lexical Function model. However, vector addition is theoretically and cognitively unsatisfactory: The meaning of a complex expression is not simply the sum of the meaning of its parts but it also depends on the syntactic content. Without being able to discriminate between the different syntactic realizations of semantic roles, sentences like

(3) a. *The dog chases the cat.*
    b. *The cat chases the dog.*

are modeled in the same way. Moreover, while vectors are suitable to capture the semantic relatedness among lexemes, this representation might not be adequate for more complex linguistic expressions because of the limited and fixed amount of information that can be encoded (Erk & Padó, 2008).

In summary, how distributional representations can be projected from the lexical level to the sentence or discourse level poses an ongoing challenge. Currently, compositionality is still considered the real bottleneck for Distributional Semantics (Lenci, 2018). It is worth highlighting that all the studies discussed earlier, in one way or another, adhere to the conventional principle of Fregean compositionality: The representation of a complex unit is derived from the representation of its immediate constituents.

A final note concerns the last generation of language models (*foundational models*, cf. Bommasani et al., 2021) built by relying on deep learning artificial neural networks and trained on massive amounts of text using a word-in-context prediction task. Numerous empirical studies have explored the compositional capabilities of neural models using various approaches (Gulordava et al., 2018; Lake & Baroni, 2018; Linzen, Dupoux, & Goldberg, 2016; Loula, Baroni, & Lake, 2018, among others). However, there is still an

Table 2 Five tests for compositionality in Neural Networks
(Hupkes et al., 2020)

Property	Test
Systematicity	If models systematically recombine known parts and rules
Productivity	If models can extend their predictions beyond the length they have seen in the training data
Substitutivity	If models' predictions are robust to synonym substitutions
Localism	If models' composition operations are local or global
Over-generalization	If models favor rules or exceptions during training

incomplete understanding of the strategies learned by these networks and their capacity to generalize. Hupkes et al. (2020) have identified five aspects of compositionality from theoretical literature (cf. Table 2) and translated them into five grounded tests for these models. This evaluation framework underscores the necessity for a more comprehensive and valid set of evaluation criteria and improved analytical tools for assessing the compositional abilities of neural networks.

2.4 Summary

This section has introduced the concept of compositionality from two distinct perspectives. First, compositionality has been outlined as a processing principle, where the fundamental assumptions and the supporting and opposing arguments have been presented. Additionally, the application of compositionality as a representation component within linguistic theory was discussed, examining its various formalizations in Formal Semantics, generative semantics, CxG, and computer science, along with their central assumptions and primary limitations.

Overall, the accounts supporting compositionality, primarily the generative approaches, propose a view of language that can be outlined in two primary components: (i) words, which are stored in a *lexicon*, and (ii) rules, which govern how words can be combined into meaningful, coherent sentences (the *grammar* component of language). The rules of grammar mostly obey the principle of compositionality: There is an inventory of rules that dictates the construction of syntactic representations, which are subsequently mapped to principles responsible for the composition of word meanings into more complex expressions. On the contrary, constructionist theories assume that there are no boundaries between lexicon and syntax, that is, between what is regular and what is irregular, or what is productive and what is unproductive. Constructions, as the basic units of language, are productive linguistic constructs that account for syntactic processes. In other words, CxG "handles 'normal syntax' in a way that necessitates a shift of perspective away from the common view of words, word classes, and phrase structure rules" (Hilpert, 2019, p. 70). While formal CxGs (e.g., SBCG, FCG, ECG) employ rigorous unification-based formalism to elucidate the emergence of well-formed structures from feature matching among their constituent parts, these approaches formalize the aggregation of constructions but do not encode other mechanisms that occur concomitantly in sentence processing.

The following section will provide behavioral evidence demonstrating that several factors affect comprehension and are against a "strong" version of compositionality centered solely on syntax-semantics homomorphism.

3 Accessing Meaning Noncompositionally: Insights from Experimental Data

This section examines (some) limitations of the Principle of Compositionality in natural language, aiming to reconcile the various bodies of literature on sentence processing. The following pages are structured in two blocks.

Section 3.1 regards what is actually included in the lexicon, a crucial aspect concerning any linguistic theory. Defining which components of a sentence are stored in long-term memory and which are constructed online in working memory is crucial to understanding and delineating the mechanisms underlying language comprehension (Jackendoff, 2002, p. 152). Thereby, Section 3.1 discusses the psycholinguistic nature of multiunit sequences, encompassing both literal and figurative meanings. Idiomatic expressions have historically served as fundamental pillars within CxG approaches, which consider idioms not mere appendages to linguistic grammar but integral entities that can be productive, highly structured, and deserving of grammatical inquiry (Fillmore, Kay, & O'Connor, 1988). Concurrently, there is a growing acceptance that multiword expressions are stored within the lexicon, particularly within the usage-based and constructionist frameworks (Abbot-Smith & Tomasello, 2006; Bybee, 2006; Goldberg, 2006). The following pages summarize mainly the experimental data about the processing of these expressions, aiming to provide (i) a cognitive validity of the CxG assumptions, and (ii) emphasis on how this definition of the lexicon is incongruent with traditional compositional approaches illustrated in Section 2.

Conversely, Section 3.2 delineates fundamental studies that support the idea that comprehension processes are often shallow, unspecified, and driven by comprehender's expectations. The hypothesis that the mental lexicon includes not only atomic representations but also an interconnected network of knowledge entails that there are multiple ways to determine meaning: People come to the task of interpretation with a vast amount of shared world knowledge and contextual information. Consequently, the semantic composition is constantly *enriched* (Jackendoff, 1997) with background knowledge and contextual constraints. Rather than undertaking a comprehensive, bottom-up analysis, interpretation may occur in a "good-enough" manner, primarily relying on expectations, potentially resulting in shallow interpretation or misinterpretation. Integrating constructional representations and principles related to this "good-enough" processing is gaining more interest and is garnering increasing attention, albeit explored in a limited number of works (Blache, 2024).

Although the behavioral evidence presented in this section aligns with the majority of constructionist perspectives, the question remains open as to how CxG could integrate shallow processing, prediction, and background knowledge into its formalism to become a comprehensive model of language processing.

3.1 Online Processing of Multiunits Sequences

3.1.1 Idioms

Idiomatic expressions are almost universally considered a challenge for compositionality (Maienborn, von Heusinger, & Portner, 2011, p. 118). Indeed, an *idiom* is traditionally defined as a phrase whose meaning cannot be deduced from its individual components (cf. Pinker, 1999). Expressions like *it's raining cats and dogs, kicked the bucket*, or *go bananas* cannot be understood by simply combining together the meaning of their constituent words; instead, their meaning must be specifically learned. For instance, there is nothing in the individual words nor the syntactic combination of "they," "chewed," "the," and "fat" that could suggest that the sentence *they chewed the fat* means that a group of people chatted (and not that the subjects actually chewed some fat). In other words, idioms do not abide by the principle of compositionality: The meanings of the parts and the rules of composition do not suffice to explain the meaning of the whole, as specific knowledge is needed.

The processing of idioms has been extensively debated in the psycholinguistic domain, and various theories have been proposed regarding whether people process idioms compositionally or holistically, that is, whether the meaning of an idiomatic phrase is stored separately from the meaning of its individual parts and how the idiomatic meaning is assembled. According to M. Libben and Titone (2008), there are approximately three different types of models of idiom processing. The "noncompositional" models contend that the whole idiomatic meaning is stored as a distinct entry in the mental lexicon and is retrieved directly as a morphologically complex word, with a process autonomous from the computation of the literal meaning. Supporters of this approach, namely, the *Lexical Representation hypothesis*, bring the empirical evidence about a processing advantage for idioms used figuratively in both comprehension and production (Gibbs, 1980; Swinney & Cutler, 1979).

On the contrary, "compositional" approaches claim that the meaning of an idiomatic phrase is not stored as a separate semantic unit in the mental lexicon but is assembled "on the fly" from the meanings of its individual parts. Therefore, analyzing each idiom's components is necessary to comprehend the idiom's figurative interpretation. For instance, Gibbs, Nayak, & Cutting (1989) posit that idiomatic expressions are represented and processed in a different way depending on whether they are decomposable, that is, the meanings of idiom components are related to the overall figurative interpretation (e.g., *pop the question*), or not (e.g., *kick the bucket*; cf. the *Idiom Decomposition hypothesis*). According to this approach, semantically decomposable expressions can be analyzed compositionally: Each component is recovered from the mental lexicon and merged with the other components based on their syntactic relationships. Conversely, the meaning of nondecomposable idioms is directly retrieved from the lexicon. Moreover, Gibbs et al. observed that sentences incorporating decomposable idioms are read more rapidly than those containing semantically nondecomposable ones. Following the assumption that decomposable idioms are processed more akin to literal language, this finding implies that an initial attempt is made to analyze idioms compositionally, as indicated by the shorter reading times for decomposable idioms. However, the results of Tabossi, Fanari, & Wolf (2009) disagree with the abovementioned hypothesis. In a semantic judgment task, participants were as fast at judging nondecomposable idioms as decomposable idioms and clichés, showing an advantage over matched controls. This study suggests that the relationship between an idiom's constituents and its overall figurative meaning does not impact its processing.

A third class regards the so-called hybrid models, which incorporate features of both noncompositional and compositional approaches. The central claim of these models is that idiomatic expressions are processed simultaneously as semantically arbitrary word sequences and compositional phrases. The *Configuration Hypothesis* of Cacciari and Tabossi (1988) is one of the most influential hybrid models. The core idea is that idiomatic phrases are processed literally, word by word, until the comprehender recognizes that the phrase they are processing is an idiom, that is, until the *idiom key* (or idiom recognition point) is reached. After this identification point, the figurative meaning is retrieved: The idiom is processed according to its figurative meaning, while compositional processing ends. In other words, once the individuals have enough information to realize that the unfolding sentence contains an idiom or an idiom fragment, such as *Tom advised them not to put all their eggs...*, they can retrieve the string from semantic memory and compare the expected constituent (*in one basket*) with the actual idiom string. Hence, the point at which the string is recognized as a known idiom determines how early the idiomatic meaning is activated. How many of the words composing the idiom string are literally processed before depends on different factors. Overall, this model strongly emphasizes the dimension of predictability to give access to the idiomatic configuration, independently of other variables, such as familiarity.

Following the Configuration Hypothesis, neurolinguistic studies have investigated how the processing advantage of idioms over nonidiomatic expressions is related to a kind of more direct access to their holistic structure once it is recognized as an idiom. Event-related potentials (ERPs)[2] studies have revealed that idiom processing correlates with faster reading time and larger electric signals in brain activity (Molinaro & Carreiras, 2010). In a well-known study, Vespignani et al. (2010) observed that the brain's electrical response to the correct idiom constituent exhibits differences when recorded before and after the idiom recognition point (RP). For instance, in the fragment

(4) *Marco piangeva sul latte*$_{RP}$ *versato* (Mark cried over the milk spilt),

the idiomatic completion elicited smaller N400 before recognition compared to other conditions (e.g., "Marco piangeva sul letto disfatto," Mark cried over the bed unmade). This observation can support the hypothesis that when we recognize a string of words as an idiom before the idiom ends, we develop expectations concerning the incoming idiomatic constituents. However, the electrophysiological response led to a P300 effect after the recognition of the idiom that was left intact, indicating the process for which the idiom meaning retrieved from long-term semantic memory must be integrated into the sentence representation to form a semantically coherent structure. This effect reflects a qualitative shift in readers' expectations regarding upcoming words once the

---

[2] Event-related potentials are a measure of the electrical activity at the scalp that occurs because of a (linguistic) stimulus, allowing us to investigate how language processing unfolds in real time. An ERP is a waveform containing a series of deflections that appear as positive/negative peaks (components) associated with functional significance. The two most studied components in linguistics are the N400, a negative wave that peaks ~400 ms after a semantically odd word is read, and P600, a positive wave that peaks ~600 ms after a syntactically odd word is read.

idiom has been recognized, indicating the activation of a template that matches the upcoming information (P300) and pointing to easier semantic integration (N400).

At the same time, Rommers et al. (2013) have shown that, during idiomatic interpretation, the literal meaning of words is actively suppressed, replaced by global access at the idiom level. This effect has been shown at the cortical level using EEG: When introducing a semantic violation within an idiom, there is no effect in processing sentences with or without semantic violations, unlike in processing literal sentences. These findings support the hypothesis that semantic unification mechanisms (i.e., integrating a word's meaning into a structure) are less engaged in idiom comprehension. In other words, the brain's semantic expectancy and literal word meaning integration operations are "switched off" when the context renders them unnecessary.

While the configuration hypothesis proposes a sequential model of idiom processing, the *Hybrid Model* (M. Libben & Titone, 2008; Titone & Connine, 1999) posits that idiom comprehension involves in parallel (i) direct meaning retrieval to figurative meaning, and (ii) compositional analysis based on the literal meanings of the idiom's constituents and syntax. The activation and use of literal or figurative meanings during comprehension is a function of the degree to which idioms are conventional or compositional: The more familiar a speaker is with an idiom, the more directly its figurative meaning can be activated and retrieved. These effects were correlated with faster and slower processing of decomposable and nondecomposable idioms, respectively. Recent studies have shown that speakers engage in a more compositional processing strategy when idioms are less frequent or familiar, for example, because they appear in a noncanonical modified form or they are being processed in a second language (Senaldi & Titone, 2022; Senaldi et al., 2022). Actually, research on idioms still investigates the various factors that can contribute to idiom processing. Among others, Cacciari, Corrardini, & Ferlazzo (2018) investigated to what extent individual differences in cognitive and personality variables are associated with spoken idiom comprehension in context.

To summarize, psycholinguistics works related to the Hybrid Model imply that, while direct retrieval of an idiomatic form is the preferential processing route, compositional (or combinatorial) parsing is present and can play a role in processing idiomatic expressions (e.g., as observed in bilingual adults; cf. Senaldi et al., 2022). Notwithstanding the extensive behavioral experiments, questions on how idioms are processed, and specifically how direct access to lexical expressions and compositional parsing interact, are still open. Indeed, the complex cognitive architecture that stands behind the comprehension of idioms has yet to be singled out in full detail.

3.1.2 Multiword Expressions

A *formulaic expression* can be broadly defined as "a sequence, continuous or discontinuous, of words or other elements, which is, or appears to be, prefabricated: that is, stored and retrieved whole from memory at the time of use" (Wray, 2002, p. 9). Formulaic language comprises many expressions commonly used in everyday language and familiar by definition. These expressions constitute a considerable portion of the language use of L1 speakers and are a reason for the fluency in production: They support the language interaction task by limiting the choices about what phrases to use when expressing particular meanings, what words to use in them, and in what order to use them (Kallens & Christiansen, 2022). In detail, formulaic language includes both literal compositional expressions as lexical bundles (*in the meantime*), verb–particle phrases (*catch up*), irreversible binomials (*bride and groom*), as well as nonliteral or figurative expressions, whose meaning is not deductible from the meaning of its components, such as the idioms already introduced.

Formulaic expressions differ from each other in several dimensions (Carrol & Conklin, 2020; Kallens & Christiansen, 2022; Siyanova-Chanturia & Sidtis, 2018; Titone et al., 2015). In general, some expressions are more "frozen" than others (fixedness/conventionalization), and they can allow for internal variation through open "slots" (schematicity). Another continuum regards compositionality, that is, how well an expression can be decomposed into atomic parts of meaning. Apart from idioms, these expressions largely vary in terms of their internal degree of compositionality: for instance, given the structurally similar collocations *carpet sweeping* and *vacuum cleaning*, the interpretation of what is being cleaned and who is cleaning is unlike (in the first case, it is the carpet that is cleaned by a brush, while in the second case something is cleaned by a vacuum; cf. Kallens & Christiansen, 2022). However, much research into these multiunit conventionalized sequences has mainly centered on how L1 speakers deal with figurative versus literal language or frequent versus novel linguistic information, usually reporting a processing advantage of recurrent sequences compared to novel control phrases (Siyanova-Chanturia & Sidtis, 2018).

In production, Bannard and Matthews (2008) observed that children repeat frequent sequences (*a drink of milk*) correctly and faster than low-frequent controls (*a drink of tea*), even if the substring frequencies are the same. Additional studies in adult comprehension replicated the same results. Among others, Arnon and Snider (2010) found that the reaction times in a phrasal decision task using four-word sequences are faster when the frequency of the whole phrase is higher: for instance, *don't have to worry* is read faster than *don't have to wait*. Moreover, they observed that this effect extends across the entire frequency range of the individual words or sub-strings. Similarly, Tremblay et al. (2011) observed that lexical bundles such as *in the middle of the* were read faster and recalled with higher accuracy than sequences matched for length such as *in the front of the* during self-paced reading experiments.

Event-related potentials and eye-tracking studies have further validated these behavioral conclusions. Tremblay and Baayen (2010) showed that the frequency of a four-word sequence continuously modulates early N1a (a peak at frontal and central sites around 100–150 msec after stimulus onset) and P1 (earliest visual ERPs potential known to vary with spatial attention, state of arousal, lexical frequency, and probability) components usually associated with frequency effects. Similar effects were replicated in English binominals. Siyanova-Chanturia, Conklin, and Schmitt (2011) observed that literal (*at the end of the day* – "in the evening") and idiomatic (*at the end of the day* – "eventually") high-frequency binomials were read faster and with fewer fixations than novel controls (*at the end of the war*) by both L1 and L2 speakers. In a recent study, Jiang et al. (2020) focused on understanding the phrase frequency effects in adults and L1 children's online processing in language comprehension by employing a naturalistic reading task (choosing Chinese as the target language). Using an eye-tracking study, they collected reading times for verb–noun combinations varying phrase frequency. As in previous literature, collocations (*attend the meeting*) were read faster than control phrases (*attend the game*). In addition, age was a significant predictor of (general) reading times across the analyses and eye-tracking measures, with the youngest (Grade 3) readers being the slowest, the oldest (adult) readers being the fastest, and Grade 4 readers being in the middle.

This frequency effect is consistent across literature, and it is typically explained in terms of storage: Language users must have some stored representation of these expressions, and they are used "holistically," even if they could be assembled by compositionally (Wray, 2012, p. 234). Conversely, compositional phrases are represented in the same way that simple words and noncompositional phrases are: The frequency of a phrase will influence its entrenchment and future processing. The difference between higher and lower-frequency phrases has to be described as a continuum (the level of activation) and not as a dichotomy (stored versus computed). Besides, Snider and Arnon (2012) support this hypothesis: Since it is hard to empirically differentiate compositional and noncompositional phrases, theories should overcome the distinction between "stored" and "computed" forms. However, what counts as the threshold for "frequent" is still an open question.

While these experiments have focused on individual types of formulaic sequences, some works have directly compared the processing of several types of phrases with different properties. For instance, Carrol and Conklin (2020) decided to compare the reading times of three types of formulaic phrases (idioms, binomials, and collocations) relative to control phrases in an eye-tracking experiment. Results revealed a processing advantage for all three types, observing that, while overall phrase frequency contributes much of the processing advantage, different phrases do show additional effects according to the specific properties relevant to each type. With the same intent, Jolsvai, McCauley, and Christiansen (2020) observed that the meaningfulness of a word sequence was an essential factor in how it was processed in a phrasal decision task, over and above simply how frequently it occurs. These observations account for a continuum between idioms and formulaic expressions: The fact that some phrases have a literal compositional and others have a figurative noncompositional meaning does not significantly affect language processing.

3.1.3 The Implications of Processing Multiwords

Evidence for the psychological reality of multiword linguistic units has served to blur the lines between grammar and lexicon, demonstrating the storage of "compositional" phrases and their use in comprehension and production (McCauley & Christiansen, 2019). In particular, idiomatic expressions and other types of multiword expressions represent an interesting test case of how the brain and the mind handle the frequency with which we are exposed to linguistic input in the environment (Cacciari, Corrardini, & Ferlazzo, 2018).

While these observations are problematic for traditional theories of language, usage-based constructionist perspectives consider these stored multiword sequences as essential building blocks for language learning and use (cf. Section 1.2). The main argument of CxG is that there is no boundary between the lexicon and the grammar: Language is a collection of constructions, form-meaning pairings varying in schematicity and complexity. Following this assumption, the dimension of the lexicon crosses the traditional representational boundaries: It includes not only idiosyncratic lexical items (i.e., words and idioms), but it comprises a large number of expressions, including partially lexicalized patterns as well as regular word forms (such as *cats, dogs*) and multiword sequences. In this respect, language could be seen as a larger store of prepackaged, or prefabricated, expressions (Bybee, 2010), which are accessed and used to comprehend and produce novel expressions. This position is shared by some models of CxG (Croft, 2001; Goldberg, 2006), which consider syntactic productivity as the extension of learned constructions. As Section 4 will introduce, the organization and productivity of language can be explained by analogical inferences from expressions stored in long-term memory rather than by sequential compositional operations (Bybee, 2010; Diessel, 2019). However, from a cognitive-processing perspective, how much repetition is required to form a linguistic chunk has yet to be established. Some multiword phrases are stored in memory, but the factors that drive this need to be clarified. Moreover, it is still critical to identify which sentences are produced using compositional mechanisms and which are not.

The implications of processing multiword units extend beyond the realm of formulaic language processing: In language processing, there is always a balance between direct memory access and compositional parsing (Senaldi & Titone, 2024). While constructionist and usage-based approaches have the merit of underlining that even structurally complex and semantically idiosyncratic units play a central role in the lexical organization and linguistic behavior, besides single words, ongoing efforts should focus on formally encoding behavioral evidence in theories and computational models of language processing.

3.2 The Predictive and Shallow Nature of Processing

3.2.1 Shallow Processing

A fundamental assumption that forms the basis of many semantic theories, particularly those supporting the principle of compositionality, is that the language processing system follows a strict and thorough syntactic algorithm to compute the representation for a given linguistic input. This tenet posits that the semantic content of words is recovered from the lexicon and subsequently combined in accordance with syntactic rules to derive the overall meaning of the sentence. However, research in psycholinguistics has provided evidence to suggest that comprehension processes frequently manifest as shallow and underspecified (Ferreira, Bailey, & Ferraro, 2002; Ferreira & Patson, 2007; Goldberg & Ferreira, 2022; Sanford & Sturt, 2002). Numerous studies reveal that syntactic structures are not always fully analyzed and exploited to extract meaning; instead, people form representations that are only "good enough" for the communicative purpose, often employing simple heuristic procedures. As a direct consequence, this process can lead to a misinterpretation of the linguistic input.

In the domains of pragmatics and psycholinguistics, several studies have revealed the existence of the so-called *semantic illusions*, a phenomenon whereby people fail to recognize an inaccuracy or inconsistency in a text. The most famous example is the well-known Moses illusion (Erickson & Mattson, 1981):

(5) *How many animals of each sort did Moses put on the ark?*

When presented with this question, subjects tend to provide the response "two" without noticing the fact that it was Noah, and not Moses, who performed the action in the biblical narrative. Comparable observations can be made to questions such as *After an air-crash, where should the survivors be buried?* (Barton & Sanford, 1993) or *Can a man marry his widow's sister?* (Sanford, 2002). These cases of lexical misinterpretation shed light on the tendency of listeners or readers to process these sentences in a superficial and shallow manner, consequently failing to detect erroneous presuppositions.

Much of the evidence for shallow processing comes from the literature on *Good-Enough Processing* (Ferreira & Lowder, 2016). This approach is based on the idea that human cognitive resources are limited, and the brain optimizes comprehension by processing language just enough to achieve understanding without engaging in overly detailed or exhaustive analysis. Good-enough processing relies on heuristics and shortcuts to comprehend language rapidly, even if it leads to occasional misinterpretations or inaccuracies.

A classic example is provided by the sentence *the dog was bitten by the man*. People often fail to compute the correct event representation, that is, the one in which the man (and not the dog) does the biting (Ferreira, 2003). Good-enough processing has mostly been investigated through the examination of garden-path sentences, such as *While Mary bathed the baby played in the crib*. Certainly, these sentences are particularly challenging to process: In this example, the noun "baby" is initially considered as the object of the verb, and it is only later in the sentence this interpretation is ruled out, replaced by a subject interpretation of the term "baby" (i.e., the baby is doing the playing and is not bathed by Mary). Christianson et al. (2001) and Ferreira, Christianson, & Hollingworth (2001) provided evidence that the correct interpretation of such utterances may not always be computed. Indeed, participants were able to correctly infer that the baby was playing in the crib. However, it was observed that they often held a confident yet incorrect belief that Mary bathed the baby. These findings emphasize that the process of garden-path reanalysis is not a binary, all-or-nothing phenomenon and suggest that the initial assignment of thematic roles for the subordinate clause verb is not invariably subject to revision (Ferreira, Christianson, & Hollingworth, 2001).

An additional example documented in the literature pertains to the phenomenon of semantic attraction. *Semantic attraction* occurs when a particular argument violates its verb's selectional requirements, yet comprehenders do not detect this violation due to its attraction to another noun within the same sentence:

(6) *The bubblegum had been chewing by the boy.*

The verb "chewing" is perceived as either syntactically or semantically anomalous. Syntactic cues suggest that the subject noun, "bubblegum," should be the Agent[3] of the verb. However, this interpretation is semantically anomalous, as inanimate objects do not typically "chew" things. Since the noun "bubblegum" is a highly plausible candidate for the Theme role of the verb, this strong semantic attraction to the Theme interpretation may lead comprehenders to pursue it, even though it contradicts the syntactic structure of the sentence (as this interpretation should require a passive verb form). In an influential study, Kim and Osterhout (2005) recorded ERPs from participants while they read sentences like those presented in this section. The authors found that sentences with attraction violations were associated with a more prominent P600 component and showed no modulations of the N400 component when compared to passive and active control sentences.

In the aforementioned cases, people tend to depend more on local linguistic information and global background knowledge rather than compositional meanings derived from fully articulated syntactic representations (McCauley & Christiansen, 2019). The reality of shallow processing challenges the prominence of hierarchical phrase structures as well as the standard generative view that syntax and semantics are consistently and autonomously processed.

3.2.2 Prediction

A complementary perspective to shallow processing is the widely shared hypothesis that "language comprehension is predictive" (Kuperberg & Jaeger, 2015, p. 1). Prediction approaches assume that efficient comprehension adopts contextual constraints to anticipate or predict upcoming input, leading to facilitated processing once the expected component is encountered (Ferreira & Lowder, 2016; Hale, 2001; Huettig, 2015; R. Levy, 2008; Pickering & Gambi, 2018; Pickering & Garrod, 2013).

From a theoretical perspective, prediction can occur at different levels, from simple priming (word meaning opens a possibility of interpreting the event) to activation. In the latter case, prediction occurs if a comprehender activates linguistic information before processing the input that carries that information. When the prediction is successful, the subject uses the pre-activated representation when encountering the linguistic chunk: In this scenario, some processing

---

[3] An Agent is the "animate and volitional initiator or doer of an action," while the Patient/Theme refers to the "entity undergoing the action and somehow affected by it" (Pustejovsky & Batiukova, 2019, p. 29). The term Patient is used to describe a receiver that changes state ("I crushed the car"), while Theme describes something that does not change state ("I have the car").

was performed at an early stage, thus explaining why prediction facilitates comprehension. This mechanism contrasts with integration, which occurs when the comprehender combines a new processed linguistic information with the representation of the preceding context (cf. Hagoort, Baggio, & Willems, 2009). In this case, facilitation effects are not witnessed in the same way, and the processing works in a bottom-up fashion. However, it can be challenging to distinguish prediction from integration and, in particular, to find evidence compatible with prediction but not integration (Pickering & Gambi, 2018). Moreover, researchers question whether the prediction mechanism is serial (it allows for the pre-activation of one highly likely candidate) or consists of the parallel pre-activation of multiple candidates (all sharing requisite semantic or orthographic features, and many options are equally likely). Admittedly, the role of prediction in language comprehension is still under debate, and the precise means by which comprehenders derive predictions still needs to be fully defined.

By exploring when information becomes available in the brain, researchers have investigated the circumstances under which people anticipate or expect upcoming input and where this predictive processing is less facilitated. Various works have demonstrated that prediction can manifest at different linguistic levels.

From a phonological perspective, DeLong, Urbach, and Kutas (2005) recorded ERPs while participants read sentences such as

(7) *The day was breezy, so the boy went outside to fly a kite/an airplane.*

The authors observed an N400 effect when the sentence ended with the less predictable *an airplane* than the more predictable *a kite*. The striking finding was that this effect occurred at the determiner *a* or *an*. This result could not be explained as a result of integration but as the prediction of the word and specifically of its phonological form (i.e., that it began with a consonant).

Predictions have been observed also at the syntactic level. Among others, Staub and Clifton (2006) found that people read *or the subway* faster after fragment (a) than after (b).

(8) a. *The team took either the train...*
    b. *The team took the train...*

The authors concluded that the conjunction *either* makes the subsequent chunk more predictable by ruling out an analysis in which *or* starts a new clause.

Indeed, there is ample evidence that contextual predictability influences lexico-semantic processing. Using the visual-world eye-tracking paradigm,

Tanenhaus et al. (1995) have shown that comprehenders actively anticipate or predict the imminent arrival of not-yet-encountered information. In this setup, subjects' eye movements are monitored as they listen to sentences while at the same time viewing an array containing pictures of various objects (e.g., *a cake, a girl, a tricycle*, and *a mouse*). Altman and Kamide (1999), in their most widely cited experiment, showed that participants directed their gaze more toward edible objects compared to inedible ones when presented with sentence fragments like *The boy will eat* (but not when the verb *eat* was replaced with other verbs, such as *move*).

The ongoing debate around prediction during sentence interpretation centers around whether the process is serial or parallel. A serial prediction approach implies that a single highly likely candidate is pre-activated, such as "bucket" in the phrase *kick the bucket*. On the other hand, a parallel approach would involve the pre-activation of multiple potential candidates when they share relevant semantic or orthographic features, and there are several equally probable options. While it is widely accepted that anticipation and prediction are integral to sentence interpretation, the specific mechanisms underlying these processes remain a subject of ongoing inquiry, together with the implementation of computational models that quantitatively define these mechanisms in relation to compositionality.

3.2.3 Background Knowledge

Lastly, psycholinguistic evidence supports the idea that knowledge of real-world events is crucial in guiding online sentence processing. For instance, the following sentence fragments

(9) a. *The doctor visits*
    b. *The veterinarian visits*

activate two different mental images and, accordingly, two different linguistic expectations. To describe this type of stored information, McRae and Matsuki (2009) have introduced the concept of *Generalized Event Knowledge* (henceforth, GEK). The term "generalized" is employed because it contains knowledge related to prototypical event types rather than detailed memory about specific event instances, differentiating from exemplar-based models (for more details on these approaches, see Section 4.2). Principally, GEK includes people's knowledge of typical participants, objects, and settings for events. This generalized knowledge about events arises from "first-hand participation, watching them on television and in movies, listening to others talk about them, and reading about them" (McRae & Matsuki, 2009, p. 1418).

Psycholinguistic and neurocognitive research has brought extensive evidence supporting that stored world knowledge plays a crucial role in online language production and comprehension. Lexical priming studies suggest that the processing of isolated words immediately activates knowledge of events of which the words are components. For instance, Ferretti, McRae, & Hatherell (2001) examined priming effects from verbs to typical agents, patients, instruments, and locations; vice versa, McRae et al. (2005) demonstrated that nouns referring to entities could prime verbs for which these nouns often serve as typical agent (*waiter-serving*), patients (*guitar-strummed*), instruments (*chainsaw-cutting*), and locations (*cafeteria-eating*). Overall, these findings on event-based priming reinforce the hypothesis that the mental lexicon is organized as an interconnected network of mutual expectations activated by the GEK (Elman, 2009, 2014).

Event knowledge influences expectations of syntactic structures, as well. McRae, Spivey-Knowlton, & Tanenhaus (1998), among others, demonstrated that the chunk *The cop arrested* tends to promote a transitive construction ("the cop arrested X") over a reduced relative structure ("the cop arrested by the X"). Conversely, the fragment *criminal arrested* promoted a reduced relative over a main verb, and reading times revealed that expectations for the syntactic continuation are affected by the status of the grammatical subject as a typical Agent (*The crook arrested by the detective was guilty*) or Patient (*The cop arrested someone*) of the main verb. Analogous observations have emerged from ERP experiments (Metusalem et al., 2012; Paczynski & Kuperberg, 2012): combinations that are more "coherent" with the event scenarios activated by the previous words result in smaller N400 amplitudes.

As a whole, these findings suggest that, during online interpretation, comprehenders tap into general knowledge regarding real-world events: Incoming linguistic input is mapped onto schemas of events, situations, or scenarios based on prior contexts or input. Therefore, the final interpretation of an utterance heavily depends on the background information. To conclude, the predictions made during language comprehension are memory-based, and one's experience about events and their participants plays a role in generating expectations about the upcoming linguistic input, thereby minimizing the overall processing effort (Elman, 2014; McRae & Matsuki, 2009).

3.2.4 Implementing Background Knowledge and Prediction

Nowadays, it is widely acknowledged that comprehenders integrate all accessible cues – contextual, semantic, and formal – to incrementally access pertinent prior linguistic and nonlinguistic representations required for interpretation

(Goldberg & Ferreira, 2022). This section illustrated numerous cases where interpretation is driven by noncompositional operations. These phenomena largely align with the main assumptions of CxG, which has directly investigated and formalized some of them.

First, constructionist approaches take into account three levels of semantic contribution for sentence interpretation: the construction, the context, and the rich background information (Michel, 2023, p. 566). As introduced in the last section, words are cues that activate event knowledge (Elman, 2009, 2011). The idea that every lexeme is interpreted against the background of a whole network of concepts in a particular domain has been formalized in *Frame Semantics* (Fillmore, 1982; Fillmore & Baker, 2010). Specifically, a *frame* is a schematic representation of an event or scenario together with the participating actors/objects/locations and their (semantic) roles. For instance, the *commercial transaction* frame includes a bulk of participant roles which must, at the very least, include *buyer, seller, goods*, and *money*. According to Fillmore, words and grammatical constructions are subordinate to frames, which means that the meaning associated with a particular word (or grammatical construction) cannot be understood independently of the frame with which it is associated. Following the previous example, verbs like *sell* and *buy* are associated with the commercial transaction frame, each representing a different perspective – one from the merchant's viewpoint and the other from the customer's. In terms of linguistic structure, frames facilitate the syntax–semantic relationship by serving as interfaces between semantic and syntactic roles, a crucial aspect in explaining noncompositional mechanisms. Nevertheless, other formalizations have been proposed to represent the meaning of constructions. For instance, Radical CxG (Croft, 2001) advocates an exemplar semantics model of the syntax–semantics mapping, in which specific situation types are organized in a multidimensional conceptual space. Formal construction types are then said to have a frequency distribution over that conceptual space.

In addition, evidence from this section aligns with the core observations of usage-based and constructionist approaches: Speakers' linguistic knowledge comes from linguistic experience, that is, lexicon and grammar are shaped by repeated exposure to specific utterances. Even more importantly, language structures at all levels, from morphology to syntax, emerge out of facts of actual language usage (Bybee, 2010), with the effect that linguistic representations are sensitive to context and statistical probabilities (Boyland, 2009).

Some theories that share some of CxG's main claims have also proposed to computationally translate these observations into quantitative and computational models. For instance, Johns and Jones (2015) introduced an exemplar model of sentence processing that uses the storage and retrieval of linguistic experiences as the fundamental operations. During the processing of new input, a vectorial representation of the sentence is used as a retrieval cue to activate past linguistic experiences, which are then used to make predictions about forthcoming words and to construct sentence meaning. Recently, Huettig, Audring, & Jackendoff (2022) developed a linguistic perspective on viewing prediction in terms of pre-activation inside the formalism of Parallel Architecture (Jackendoff, 1997, 2002), which share similar assumptions about language with the constructionist approaches (Jackendoff, 2013). On a theoretical note, Michel (2023) suggested the use of Predictive Processing as a cognitive-computational paradigm for CxG. On a related note, it is worth mentioning that there is a growing body of research that addresses language comprehension and language production from a constructional point of view. However, the focus has mostly been on argument structure constructions, with few attempts on morphological constructions or information structure constructions (Hilpert, 2019, p. 153).

In summary, behavioral evidence regarding language comprehension largely aligns with the fundamental tenets of CxG. Nonetheless, while primary literature in CxG has focused on formalizing linguistic representations, only recent works have endeavored to elucidate the operational mechanisms within the theoretical framework of CxG, with even fewer studies attempting computational implementations (cf. Section 5.4). The review hereby proposed suggests that there is a need for further efforts to elucidate the interplay among diverse sources of information and to delineate the fundamental mechanisms to (i) access to the meaning of constructions and (ii) combine constructions and other sources of information into the final interpretation.

3.3 Summary

All the experimental literature summarized in this section poses against a serial account of sentence processing where syntax proposes a structural interpretation for semantics to cash out subsequently.

First, the evidence for the psychological reality of multiword linguistic units points to a linguistic model in which there is no clear boundary between expressions stored in our memory and expressions generated by compositional mechanisms, as claimed by constructionist approaches: The large number of facilitation effects observed in language processing make us doubt a clear way to distinguish different processes for idiomatic, formulaic, and novel expressions. While this is problematic for a strong view of compositionality, the notion of constructions and the importance of frequency in modeling semantic memory implies a redefinition of *what* linguistic units are combined and *how* they are combined to provide the final representation of a sentence.

Secondly, language processing can be seen as a process predominantly driven by sequence matching and pattern identification and incorporates probabilistic cues, including, importantly, the frequency and predictability of the sentence and its component. Compositionality, devised as a mechanism to aggregate meaning, should be redefined as a complex mechanism able to integrate a network of activated linguistic and contextual information.

Altogether, a linguistic theory of language processing should provide a formalization that (i) integrates formal, semantic, and contextual knowledge, and (ii) implements the predictive nature of comprehension and quantitatively models the basic processing of the good-enough approach, that is, the *"interpret whenever possible"* principle. Among others, Blache (2017) proposed that, instead of building a syntactic structure serving as support of the comprehension of a sentence, the processing mechanism is delayed until enough information becomes available (i.e., the density of information – or the cohesion – reaches a certain threshold). This general parsing mechanism offers the possibility to integrate different sources of information when they become available by delaying the evaluation, waiting until a certain threshold of cohesion can be identified.

4 Explaining Productivity through Analogy

So far, we have discussed various cases in which the principle of compositionality is suppressed in place of noncompositional access to meaning. While the focus has primarily centered on the cognitive processing of highly frequent and predictable linguistic expressions, an equally fundamental aspect to consider pertains to the generation of novel constructs. Indeed, any theory, even the most hostile to compositional processes governed by online rules, must necessarily account for the production and comprehension of sentences conveying novel events and concepts. Consequently, notwithstanding the assumption that the semantics of multiword sequences can be held in our long-term memory, thereby facilitating predictive comprehension, it remains necessary to elucidate the mechanisms that enable the generation of entirely novel, never-encountered-before linguistic structures.

The generative tradition has claimed that linguistic knowledge constitutes a separate cognitive faculty, informationally encapsulated and structured according to its specific principles (Hauser, Chomsky, & Fitch, 2002). Within this framework, compositionality is regarded as an innate constraint of this faculty of language, governing the meaning-determining operations (Del Pinal, 2015).

However, the usage-based constructionist perspectives challenge this idea, claiming that language is no different from any other cognitive domain. Linguistic structures do not result from a specific language function but rather can be explicable as the manifestation of domain-general processes, including categorization, chunking, rich memory storage, crossmodal association, and analogy (Bybee, 2010, p. 7). Consequently, these paradigms advocate an alternative approach to address creativity and productivity in language (cf. Section 1.3), rooted in a specific domain-general process, namely, analogy (Bybee, 2010).

Analogical reasoning is recognized as a potent cognitive device that allows one to discover similarities, formulate conceptual categories, and extrapolate them to novel categorical domains (Behrens, 2017). In its broadest sense, analogy denotes the ability to think about relational patterns (Holyoak, Gentner, & Kokinov, 2001, p. 2). The concept of analogy holds a central position in contemporary cognitive science and is considered a fundamental mechanism in human cognition. Notably, Hofstadter emphasizes the cardinal role of analogy by likening it to the "motor of the car of thought" and "the interstate freeway of cognition," designating it as "the core of human cognition" (Hofstadter, 2009).

This section will introduce the concept of analogy as a cognitive process employed within the domain of cognitive science. The specific definitions and the explanation of its main characteristics are essential to understanding how to insert analogical operations in a model of language processing coherent with cognitive observation. Subsequently, it will introduce how usage-based constructionist approaches have proposed analogy as a mechanism of language, with a specific focus on the role of analogy in language productivity. Additionally, there will be summarized how analogy was computationally implemented in cognitive and distributional models.

4.1 Analogical Reasoning and Its Role in Cognition

Analogy is a domain-general cognitive process that enables a structure mapping between two situations or objects (Gentner, 1983). In the most typical case, a familiar concrete domain, referred to as the *base* or *source*, functions as a template by which one can understand and draw new inferences about a less familiar or abstract domain, namely the *target* (Gentner & Smith, 2013).

Analogical thinking is pervasive in human thought and speech. People draw on experiential analogies to form mental models of phenomena in the world every day. One example is the often-cited "Rutherford analogy": A sentence like *The atom is like the solar system* is acceptable because some aspects of the structure of the atom (notably the fact that electrons orbit the nucleus) can be understood from prior knowledge of the structure of the solar system (i.e., planets orbit the sun).

Over the last three decades, Gentner and colleagues have conducted an extensive investigation into analogy, developing one of the most influential frameworks in cognitive research. The *Structure-Mapping Theory* of analogy (Gentner, 1983, 1988; Gentner & Markman, 1997) delineates the set of implicit constraints by which people interpret analogy and similarity. At its core, the theory posits that analogy is characterized by mapping relations between objects, rather than attributes of objects, from base to target. Accordingly, the theory assesses analogies on purely structural grounds, as defined by Falkenhainer, Forbus, and Gentner (1989, p. 3): "This structural view of analogy is based on the intuition that analogies are about relations, rather than simple features. No matter what kind of knowledge (causal models, plans, stories, etc.), it is the structural properties (i.e., the interrelationships between the facts) that determine the content of an analogy."

Going back to the Rutherford analogy, the sentence *The atom is like the solar system* is interpretable as "The electron revolves around the nucleus, just as the planets revolve around the sun." However, the atom and the sun do not share the same features; that is, the analogy does not imply that "The nucleus is *yellow, massive*, etc., like the sun"). If that were the case, we would have a *literal similarity* statement instead, in which a large number of both object attributes and relational predicates are mapped from base to target relative to the number (Gentner, 1983). In other words, the two situations are analogous because they share the complex relationship known as "to revolve around"; however, the target object does not have to resemble its corresponding base.

Analogical processes, hence, rely on a structure-mapping engine (SME) that identifies relations between representations rather than the mere similarity between their attributes. In this sense, mapping of one entity to another depends on the "syntactic properties of the knowledge representation [describing the entities], and not on the specific content of the domains" (Gentner, 1983, p. 1). To clarify, this process is not triggered simply by surface similarity but requires a great deal of relational or structural alignment knowledge:

> Analogy occurs when comparisons exhibit a high degree of relational similarity with very little attribute similarity. As the amount of attribute similarity increases, the comparison shifts toward literal similarity. (Gentner & Markman, 1997, p. 48)

Figure 3 provides a concrete illustration of these differences. On the one side, (perceptual) similarity occurs when an observer perceives the resemblance

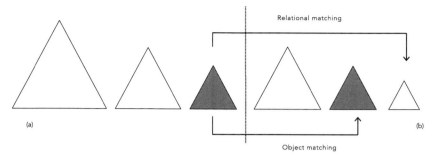

Figure 3 Perceptual similarity and relational analogy

Note: The smallest triangle in (a) could match either with the middle triangle in (b) – applying an object match, or with the rightmost triangle – following a relational match.
Source: Adapted from Gentner and Smith (2012, p. 131).

between two objects, such as the medium-sized triangle in (b) and the smallest triangle in (a), which are identical in size. In this case, the two objects match because they share identical perceptible attributes. In contrast, the analogy between the smallest triangle in (a) and the small one in (b) is based on a relational resemblance: While these objects differ in size, they both hold the distinction of being the smallest within their respective sets. However, it is crucial to bear in mind that the demarcation between analogy and similarity is not a strict dichotomy; rather, it exists along a continuum.

Since the late 1980s, cognitive works have converged to delineate the general characteristics of analogical thinking across domains. Most theorists agree that analogies can be decomposed into several basic component processes. Specifically, Gentner and Smith (2013, p. 670) identify three key stages involved in analogical reasoning.

- **Retrieval**: In this stage, the individual retrieves information from their long-term memory (*base*) based on a current topic or situation they are dealing with in the working memory (*target*). The goal is to find a prior analogous situation or case from their memory that is similar in some way to the current situation. This retrieval of past experiences or knowledge is essential for drawing parallels and making analogies.
- **Mapping**: Once a relevant analogous situation has been retrieved, the mapping stage involves aligning and comparing the representations of the base and the target. This alignment process helps identify similarities, differences, and relationships between the elements or components of the two cases. It also allows for projecting inferences from one situation to the other. This mapping process is systematic and structure-consistent, meaning it considers the larger relational systems within the cases.

- **Evaluation**: After the analogical mapping is complete, the individual evaluates the analogy and its associated inferences. This evaluation can involve assessing the validity and relevance of the analogy to the current situation. It also includes judging the quality and reliability of the inferences drawn from the analogy. Effective evaluation is crucial for making informed decisions or solving problems based on the analogical reasoning process.

Holyoak (2012) offers an accurate summary of the strategies underlying analogical thinking (p. 10):

> In a typical reasoning scenario, one or more relevant analogs stored in long-term memory must be *accessed*. A familiar analog must be *mapped* to the target analog to identify systematic correspondences between the two, thereby aligning the corresponding parts of each analog. The resulting mapping allows analogical *inferences* to be made about the target analog, thus creating new knowledge to fill gaps in understanding. These inferences need to be evaluated and possibly *adapted* to fit the unique requirements of the target. Finally, in the aftermath of analogical reasoning, *learning* can result in the generation of new categories and schemas, the addition of new instances to memory, and new understandings of old instances and schemas that allow them to be accessed better in the future.

To summarize, analogical reasoning is not just comparing two analogs based on the similarities we perceive. Instead, it is a complex process of retrieving structured knowledge from long-term memory, representing and manipulating role-filler bindings in working memory, generating new inferences, and finding structured intersections between analogs to form new abstract schemata (Holyoak, 2012). Besides, an aspect that is generally highlighted is that analogy is an active process that can shape our perception, and it is a central component to learning and transfer.

According to Gentner and Smith (2012), analogical processes can augment and extend knowledge in four ways. In *inference projection*, spontaneous candidate inferences are made from a well-structured representation to one that is not entirely complete. *Schema abstraction*, instead, is abstraction of shared relational structure across different exemplars. This structure may be stored in memory as an abstraction and used again for later exemplars. In *difference detection*, the structural alignment process highlights alignable discrepancies between analogs and makes them more salient. Finally, new representations could be made by relying on *re-representation*: Even when two potential analogs have nonidentical conceptual relations, they may still be analogous if altering one or both analog representations improves the relational match.

In that sense, analogical reasoning leads to learning in terms of categorization, abstraction, and category extension: "The cognizer needs the ability to compare two structures and notice discrepancies as well as similarity or over-lap. When source and target (the new item) match in the relevant respects, the target is categorized as an item belonging to the source category" (Langacker, 1999, p. 4). Gentner, Holyoak, Hofstadter, and numerous other scholars have conducted extensive research on the role of analogy in the process of learn-ing, substantiating their investigations with insights from psychology and, more recently, neurology.

In brief, analogy can be defined as "an inductive mechanism based on structured comparisons of mental representations" (Holyoak, 2012, p. 1). More broadly, analogical thinking plays a crucial role in creative discovery, problem-solving, categorization, learning, and knowledge transfer. A funda-mental aspect of research is its interdisciplinary nature, allowing multiple fields to contribute collectively to our comprehension of cognitive processes. Psychological experiments, naturalistic observations, linguistic analyses, and computer simulations offer diverse perspectives on analogy. For the present discussion, the following section provides an overview of how the analogi-cal mechanism has been proposed as an explanation of language production in linguistic theory.

4.2 Analogy in Language Use

Considerable evidence from cognitive psychology underscores the pivotal role of analogical reasoning as a foundational element of human cognition. Con-sequently, it is not surprising that analogy has been recognized as a core component of linguistic competence from the earliest times (Blevins & Blevins, 2009). In linguistics, the mechanism of analogy has been conceptualized as a principle governing regularities in language, mostly behind morphologi-cal regularization (Anttila, 1977; Hock, 2003, among others). However, this process has gained renewed attention within usage-based and construction-ist approaches, which regard analogy as a fundamental mechanism behind language development and productivity (cf. Behrens, 2017 for a systematic review).

As already mentioned, analogical reasoning involves a structural mapping process, wherein parallel structures are aligned to draw inferences about the less familiar structures based on knowledge derived from a more familiar coun-terpart. Due to the intrinsic relational nature of language, it is possible to align and map identical or similar linguistic structures to which speakers have been exposed (Holyoak, 2012). Consequently, introducing a novel element within a linguistic construction requires a great deal of relational or structural alignment knowledge and substantial similarity to existing elements, thereby

Table 3 Analogy-based versus rule-based approaches in language processing (cf. Bybee, 2010, pp. 73–74)

	Analogy	**Rules**
Pattern usage	Relies on stored constructions or lexical items	Abstract and independent of specific instances
Productivity	Influenced by the number of participant items they can apply to Productivity seen as gradient	Determined by "default" status (i.e., used in typical situations) Rules viewed as either productive or unproductive
Relation to existing types	Highly influenced by existing types	Applies to entire categories without consideration for their individual items
Probabilistic nature	Probabilistic – individual types may vary in their closeness to the best exemplars of a category	Discrete – conforms to a rule or does not
Relation to meaning	Constructions relate meaning to form and are grounded in linguistic and extralinguistic contexts	Typically viewed as purely syntactic, no inherent connection to meaning

departing from a strong rule-governed view of productivity (cf. Table 3). The commonalities of the two structures could also generate an abstraction (or generalization) of these patterns. The following pages explore previous approaches to analogy-based productivity.

According to the constructionist view, language is a large repository of constructions with several levels of abstraction, from specific expressions to general patterns (Dąbrowska, 2017). However, novel utterances also occur. The question is then to understand what role our ample stored knowledge has in language productivity (and creativity, if possible). The argument proposed is that, even when we create novel expressions, people exploit the similarity with already encountered, stored sequences: Some new expressions are "more similar" to existing prefabs, and some are more remote to them. The term analogy is then used to identify the mechanism that, given a new sequence, determines the pattern that best serves as a foundation on which a speaker might articulate new linguistic forms (Ambridge, 2020a; Bybee, 2010; Diessel, 2019). According to this view, the organization and productivity of language are the result of analogies between form and/or meaning in a structured inventory of constructions (Ibbotson, 2013), or, in other words:

> Analogy is the process by which novel utterances are created based on previously experienced utterances. (Bybee, 2010, p. 8)

The notion of analogy as a mechanism driving productivity has been explored in various linguistic domains.

Several examples are found in morphology, where substantial evidence suggests that new formations consistently rely on similarity to existing exemplars (Bybee, 2010). Among others, a great deal of research has focused on an apparent simple morphological phenomenon: English past-tense marking. The general idea of these works is that speakers do internalize rules, but these rules are few and cover only regular processes; the remaining patterns are attributed to analogy (Pinker & Prince, 1988). A series of studies involving acceptability judgments and production, conducted with both adults (Albright & Hayes, 2003) and children (Ambridge, 2010; Blything, Ambridge, & Lieven, 2018), revealed that both the acceptability and the likelihood of producing "regular" past-tense forms for a novel verb (e.g., *wiss, bredged, chooled, daped*) are determined by the phonological similarity of the verb to existing stored "regular" past-tense forms (e.g., *wissed* being similar to *missed, hissed, and wished*; cf. Ambridge, 2020a, p. 520). The same pattern holds for "irregular" forms (e.g., *flept* being similar to *slept, wept*, and *crept*), as it was also observed by Bybee and Moder (1983).

In word formation, analogy is described as the process of creating a new word, patterned after an existing one, such as the formation of *software* after *hardware* ("surface analogy"; cf. Mattiello, 2017). Of the various word formation processes, compound words represent one of the most studied phenomena, as the productivity of compounding is considerably greater than other word formation processes. Recently, Mattiello (2016; 2017) studied novel analogical compounds in English, where words are formed either through a specific model (e.g., *beefcake* after *cheesecake*) or a schema model (e.g., *green-collar* after *white-collar, blue-collar, pink-collar*, and other similar compounds).

There is also a large amount of literature in psycholinguistics that has investigated the production, representation, and processing of compounds by means of analogical inferences (cf. Krott, 2009 for an introduction). For instance, Coolen, Van Jaarsveld, and Schreuder (1991) suggest that "the interpretability of isolated novel compounds may be determined by the availability of lexicalized compounds that can serve as a model for the interpretation" and the "[r]elations within these lexicalized compounds may be among the first ones that are considered in the interpretation process" (p. 350). Research by Christine Gagné and colleagues (see, for example, Gagné, 2001; Gagné & Shoben, 1997) highlights that the frequency of how compound constituents are used in existing compounds with similar interpretations affects how a new compound is interpreted. For example, when presented with the novel compound *honey soup* (interpreted as "a soup made of honey"), people read it faster if it is preceded by a compound with the same relation, like *honey muffin* ("a muffin made of honey") compared to when it is preceded by a compound with a different relation, such as *honey insect* ("a honey made by insect(s)"). Notably, this phenomenon occurs only when the prime and target compounds share a common modifier (Gagné, 2001).

Behavioral evidence points toward a model of compounding that is far from classic rule-based morphology: "New compound words rarely are formed de novo from two independent words. Rather, they are created through a process of partial analogy in which one element of an existing compound is exchanged" (G. Libben, 2014, p. 15). Overall, the compounds seem to invite individuals to search their memories for experiences with exemplars of the referents being identified by a compound and to create a new, ad hoc, category for it on the spot based on the examples found in memory (Chandler, 2017).

At the construction level, some works in CxG have presented evidence about the importance of prior constructions in producing novel combinations; that is, the meaning of a new sequence can derive from an extension of the meaning of a learned construction (Diessel, 2019; Goldberg, 2019; Hilpert, 2019). For instance, Boas (2003, pp. 260–284) usees the term "analogical creativity" to argue that the creative use of verbs in novel syntactic contexts could be explained by "item-based analogy," driven by local similarities between particular verbs. For instance, given the sentence "She sneezed the napkin off the table," a speaker can associate the resultative meaning stemming from the conventionalized [NP V NP XP] syntactic frame of *blow* (the source) with *sneeze* (the target). This position is in line with Goldberg's view on the productivity of construction, whose focus includes the impact of type frequency and the coherence of a constructional schema and others (Goldberg, 2019). Let us consider another example. The meaning of the Ditransitive construction is closely connected with "transfer of possession" as in *John gave Mary a goat*. Metaphorical extensions of this pattern, such as *John gave the goat a kiss* or even *Cry me a river*, are understood by analogy to the core meaning of the construction from which they were extended, which in the case of the ditransitive is something like "X causes Y to receive Z" (Goldberg, 2006). Goldberg (2019, pp. 63–64) directly refers to the theory proposed by Gentner and colleagues: "The formal surface regularities of constructions invite learners to seek other types of regularities across exemplars, through a process of *structural alignment*, which we recall involves relating two (or more) distinct relational structures."

In addition, Goldberg stated that by aligning the abstract relational structure of, for instance, *I love you* and *You want a cookie*, the shared relational structure, "animate entity experiences attitude toward something," becomes more salient, and also the individual differences stand out (e.g., a pronoun object versus a lexical noun phrase object; (Goldberg, 2019, p. 64)).

To summarize, the usage-based constructionist approach relies on the fact that learners attend to and retain aspects of both the form and interpretation of utterances. This assumption leads to clustering the instances of constructions in the hyper-dimensional space we use to represent language so that more general constructions can emerge. In other words, the process of aligning exemplars relies on both formal properties and the meaning of the exemplars.

A final consideration that must be accounted for regards the risk of approaching language productivity as only and exclusively determined by stored exemplars and analogy. Indeed, the notion that we store direct linguistic experience and use it to understand a novel expression is comparable to *exemplar models of language*. Exemplar-based approaches provide both a model of how language is represented and how learning and using language takes place.

Combining exemplar models with the mechanism of analogy as the driving process of productivity can lead, in its most extreme version, to a complete repudiation of any form of abstraction, considering concrete (i.e., experienced) exemplars as the only stored elements. According to Ambridge (2020a), forms of which one has never had direct experience are produced and understood through on-the-fly analogical processes with respect to multiple stored exemplars and weighed according to their degree of similarity to the new instance, without reference to any kind of abstraction (such as the concepts of [VERB] [NAME], [SUBJECT], etc.). Chandler (2017) has supported a similar position (p. 81):

> [O]ur knowledge of linguistic categories, and perhaps of language more generally, does not consist of resident linguistic generalizations, a grammar, that have been abstracted away from our experiences with exemplars of linguistic usage. Instead, the phenomena of categories and of categorization appear to be better explained by positing a mechanism and a set of procedures by which we compare current instances of linguistic usage systematically to memories for previous instances of similar usages in order to arrive at a formulation or interpretation of the new instance on the fly.

However, the ensuing discussion (see Ambridge, 2020b) showed the profound difficulties with such a view; namely, abstraction is necessary for the psychologically realistic storage of linguistic experiences. The version proposed by Goldberg in the CxG framework is more realistic than a radical exemplar-based view of language. While we can affirm that we memorize more linguistic units of language, human brain architecture is shaped to generalize from single items of experience: "language processing requires that our brains recode and compress incoming information. Thus memory traces of experiences, no matter how vivid, are partially abstracted from our experience" (Goldberg, 2019, p. 16). In that sense, Ambridge's radically exemplar model is not coherent with our cognitive architecture.

COMMON ASSUMPTIONS OF EXEMPLAR-BASED MODELS
Adapted from Kaplan (2017)

- **Concrete Instances, Not Abstract Concepts** Linguistic knowledge is not founded on abstract generalizations; rather, it is rooted in a multitude of specific linguistic encounters or *exemplars*.
- **Exemplars as Structured Entities** Exemplars consist of rich linguistics and extralinguistic information recorded from experience.
- **Emergence of Grammar from Exemplar Clusters** Categories and grammatical units can emerge from the experience recorded in memory. Exemplars are categorized by similarity to one another, showing prototype effects; generalizations about words and grammatical categories thus arise from the central tendencies within the clusters of exemplars associated with them.

4.3 Analogy in Computational Models of Language

Several approaches within the domain of artificial intelligence (AI) have been proposed to replicate abstraction and analogy-making in computational systems. These strategies range from earlier symbolic or hybrid approaches, like Gentner et al.'s structure-mapping approach and the "active symbol" approach of Hofstadter and colleagues (Hofstadter, 1985; Hofstadter & Mitchell, 1994), to recent techniques employing deep neural networks and probabilistic program induction (see M. Mitchell, 2021 for a complete review). Among others, structure mapping theory has been translated into computational form through the *Structure Mapping Engine* (SME) (Falkenhainer, Forbus, & Gentner, 1989; Forbus et al., 2017). Structure Mapping Engine's input consists of descriptions of two entities or situations, a base and a target, each consisting of a set of logical propositions. This model primarily focuses on the mapping process of analogy-making; thus, the situations to be mapped have already been represented in a logical form. Structure Mapping Engine provides a domain-independent explanation of analogy-making, concentrating on mapping the structure or syntax of its input representations rather than delving into domain-specific semantics. The challenge arises from the fact that human mental representations of real-world situations (including linguistic knowledge) are typically not as rigidly segmented as required by this architecture.

In the linguistic domain, at least three exemplar-based computational models have been proposed to replicate analogy in the realm of phonological, morphological, and lexical usage: Nosofsky's *Generalized Context Model* (Nosofsky, 1990), Daelemans's *Tilburg Memory Based Learning Model* (Daelemans & Van Den Bosch, 2010), and Skousen's *Analogical Model* (Skousen, 1989). These models share the assumption that we recognize and interpret the significance of present experiences by directly comparing them with memories of past experiences. This approach involves specific memories rather than schematized representations abstracted from those collective experiences. Consequently, each of the three exemplar-based models suggests a continuous accumulation of rich sensory memories over an individual's life, along with a procedure for comparing the sensory input of a current experience with the stored representations of one or more of those earlier experiences (Chandler, 2017).

Analogical Modeling (AM) (Skousen, 1989, 1992) seems to be fully compatible with our present comprehension of the psychological abilities and functions governing categorization behavior (Chandler, 2017). This model is based on the idea that past linguistic experiences are stored within the mental lexicon. When the need arises to analyze certain linguistic behaviors (such as pronunciation, morphological relationships, words, etc.), the lexicon itself is accessed. The process involves searching for the stored exemplars that closely resemble the one whose behavior is being predicted. Typically, the behavior of highly similar stored entities predicts the behavior of the one in question, although less similar ones also have a small probability of being applicable.

In detail, AM comprises three main components: (i) the dataset, which consists of exemplars accumulated in long-term memory and used as a basis for performing analogical operations on a current target form; (ii) the core of the AM, an algorithm designed to select from the dataset the exemplar(s) serving as the basis for analogically interpreting the target form; and (iii) decision rule(s) used to choose one or more forms in the analogical set, determining the basis for the analogical interpretation of the target form. In the process of classifying a target form, AM takes into account all exemplars that share certain features with the target (*supracontext*). However, only those that do not add uncertainty to the classification (*homogeneity*) are chosen for the final list, namely, the analogical set. Ambridge (2020a, p. 521) provides an example of how AM works:

> For example, if the target is the novel verb chool (from Albright & Hayes, 2003), the analogical set contains *choose* (→*chose*) and *chew* (→*chewed*), which narrow down the choice of classification (to either *chool*→*chole* or *chool*→*chooled*). It does not include, for examples, cheat, check, cheer, poop, puke or boot because, although each shares one or more feature with the target, they serve only to increase uncertainty regarding classification.

While these models have allowed linguists to test the claims and implications of the exemplar approach explicitly against both observationally and experimentally obtained data, none of the three exemplar models has yet been applied to the incremental syntactic interpretation of word strings. Recently, Chandler (2020), in its commentary to Ambridge (2020a), illustrated how to apply AM incrementally to the ambiguous sentence such as *They fed her dog biscuits*, arguing that a similar computational model could test Ambridge's hypothesis empirically (p. 571). Within the field of language acquisition, Bod (2009) demonstrated how a computational learning algorithm is able to employ structural analogy in a probabilistic way. This process mimicked children's language development, going from item-based constructions to abstract constructions, even simulating some errors witnessed in children producing complex questions.

A final consideration regards how the mechanism of analogy can be modeled in Distributional Models (introduced in Section 2.3). Word analogies have been used as a standard intrinsic evaluation task for measuring the quality of word (O. Levy & Goldberg, 2014; Linzen, Dupoux, & Goldberg, 2016; Mikolov, Yih, & Zweig, 2013) and sentence embeddings (Ushio et al., 2021, Wang, Daille, & Hathout, 2021; Zhu & de Melo, 2020). However, the task is usually defined as a candidate retrieval: Given a pair of words (*Tokyo, Paris*) and a third one (*Paris*), the goal is to identify the underlying relation behind the first pair (IS THE CAPITAL OF) and find the correct completion from a list of candidates to solve the analogy (*France*, in this case). However, a different perspective has been brought from works in visual analogy and deep learning techniques in the last few years. Researchers in computer vision (Ichien et al., 2021; Reed et al., 2015; Sadeghi, Zitnick, & Farhadi, 2015; Upchurch, Snavely, & Bala, 2016) have built deep-learning neural network architectures that organize visual representations in the same way as distributional semantic vector spaces organize linguistic data. These works consisted of recognizing a visual relationship between two images and generating a transformed query image accordingly. Among others, Reed et al. (2015) developed a novel deep network that was trained to perform visual analogies, transforming an image in the same way shown by a pair of example images. For instance, given a 3D image of a car in a frontal pose and its left-rotated version, the network should replicate the same rotation for another object, for example, a truck. What is relevant for language is that this model is directly trained on the objective of analogy completion, that is, it generates an appropriate image to make a valid analogy. Recently, Rambelli et al. (2022) proposed a neural network simulating the construction of phrasal embedding as an analogical process by taking inspiration from word embeddings and computer vision techniques. The authors proposed an analogical model to create the distributional embeddings of new expressions by applying a variant of Reed et al.'s network and evaluated different architectures in terms of generalization and systematicity.

To conclude, current computational models of analogical inference in language are still rather rudimentary, and we are nowhere near possessing a model that captures not only the statistical abilities of speakers but also their preferences and limitations.

4.4 Summary

The present section introduced the cognitive mechanism of analogy in the debate on mechanisms of language processing. First, it delineated the main characteristics of analogy. While a comprehensive review of analogy in cognitive science might appear excessive, the primary objective is to inform the reader about the true nature of analogy, and the specific characteristics of this cognitive process. Indeed, a thorough description of the mechanisms of analogy could be beneficial for those who aim to incorporate analogy into a linguistic model.

Subsequently, it illustrated the usage-based rationales that support the proposition that analogical processing constitutes the basis of the human ability to create novel utterances. Specifically, the main assumption is that the interpretation of a novel linguistic expression can be derived from stored word sequences, which function as analogical bases. While this perspective has been successfully adopted in recent studies of language acquisition, we agree with Bybee's thesis that analogy could also be applied in adult production to account for novel utterances. The notion of analogy as a mechanism behind language processing has profound implications for linguistic theory, as it attenuates the role of compositionality. For instance, a transparent sentence like *reading a papyrus* could be understood in analogy with stored the frequent expression *reading a book* (Rambelli et al., 2022) instead of assembling the meaning of the lexemes (which is, however, still possible). Consequently, examples of language productivity could be explained by analogical inferences rather than by sequential compositional operations. The question of which mechanism (combinatorial or analogical) takes place in a given moment is an open question the author is still interested in exploring.

The section also included a review of analogical models to underscore the necessity of implementing a computational model designed to process sentence-level constructions, raising the question of how to incorporate analogical mechanisms into this architectural framework.

5 Rethinking Compositionality: A Constructionist Perspective

As we discussed at the beginning of this Element, compositionality is perhaps one of the most potent and well-defended tenets in theoretical linguistics, and for good reason. Indeed, compositionality explains why it is possible to easily comprehend the meaning of a new sentence. Generative tradition has operationalized this concept starting from the assumption that sentences are generated by syntax; thus, semantic composition must follow syntactic composition in every step, from combining individual words into phrases to combining phrases into a sentence (Dowty, 2007; Szabó, 2012). In that sense, the interpretation of a sentence depends on the hierarchical syntactic structure alone, and representations formed during this process are accurate, precise, and detailed (cf. Section 2).

Conversely, usage-based constructionist approaches refuse the strict view of compositionality (or *simple composition*, cf. Culicover & Jackendoff, 2006; Jackendoff, 1997), focusing more on (i) the cognitive abilities involved in compositionality and (ii) the idea that compositionality is just one aspect of the diverse mechanisms of combinatoriality in human language and cognition (Pleyer, Lepic, & Hartmann, 2022). These approaches often assume that compositionality is not a singular concept explaining all forms of meaningful combination in a communication system; rather, human language also includes noncompositional mechanisms of combination. These positions are sustained by behavioral evidence from psycholinguistic literature: language processing is often under-specified, linguistic information comes from different and heterogeneous sources that may vary depending on usage, and prediction is crucial for efficient language comprehension (cf. Section 3). Therefore, it is not necessarily true that syntactic structure fully determines meaning composition. Interpretation derives from the combination of bottom-up and top-down strategies, and it is an empirical issue of how syntax contributes to meaning composition precisely. Moreover, by defining the language system not as an innate faculty with its own rules, but as a system governed by general cognitive processes, more mechanisms could underlie language comprehension, such as the analogical process (cf. Section 4).

In light of these observations, it becomes necessary to revisit the question: *What is compositionality?* In order to provide an accurate answer, it is imperative to distinguish between two conceptualizations of compositionality: First, as a property inherent to language (and cognition), and secondly, as a linguistic principle governing the aggregation of meaning from stored units into larger (and typically innovative) utterances. Moreover, the constructionist redefinition of compositionality as a processing principle carries significant implications for the construction of a model of language comprehension. Toward the conclusion of this section, a recent proposition in this regard will be examined.

5.1 Redefining Compositionality as a Property of Natural Language

A common assumption is that human thought and language are compositional by nature (Martin & Baggio, 2020). By specifically posing the problem that way, this statement implies that both the language of thoughts and natural language are intrinsically compositional. The relationship between language and thought is vast and particularly controversial, and this Element is not interested in entering this debate. Generally, an influential assumption is that thought is mainly prior to and independent of linguistic communication: It is the system of thought (semantics) that shapes language. The connection between language and thought has been examined by Jerry Fodor, who has claimed that just thought, and not language, is compositional. Addressing the question of which precedes the other – thought or language – he proposed that at least one of them must be compositional, and if only one is compositional, that is the one that has underived semantic content. Fodor suggested that if natural languages lack compositionality, their content then derives from the content of thought (Fodor, 2001, p. 234).

From a different field of study, Christiansen and Chater (2016a) mentioned that "compositionality, function argument structure, quantification, aspect, and modality are properties of the thoughts that language may express" (p. 51). In this perspective, if thoughts are compositional, then the language should be itself compositional. However, it seems more accurate to say that there is a "capacity" for compositional processing and representation in our mind, which is recruited and expressed in language (Baggio, 2020, p. 5). Analogously, the usage-based perspectives support the hypothesis that cognitive processes shape language. From this stance, the problem can be rephrased as follows: As we can aggregate concepts, we somehow apply this cognitive mechanism to linguistic processing.

This assumption yields a reformulation of what we mean when saying "language is compositional." For instance, Dowty (2007) proposes to apply the term natural language compositionality "to whatever strategies and principles we discover that natural languages actually do employ to derive the meanings of sentences, on the basis of whatever aspects of syntax and whatever additional information (if any) research shows that they do in fact depend on" (p. 6). In other words, it is one of the possible strategies used to explain productivity, but it is not the only one. A different position is represented by Baggio's works. The author still considers compositionality a backbone of language; however, his idea has less to share with the traditional Fregean compositionality. For instance, Baggio, Van Lambalgen, & Hagoort (2012) claimed that the real issue about compositionality and open-ended productivity in natural language is "the balance between storage and computation." While the centrality of compositionality is diminished, it is evident that human languages have algorithms for building meanings from their parts (Călinescu, Ramchand, & Baggio, 2023). The open question is so when this computational constraint occurs and modulates language processing. One possibility is that "compositionality can often be rescued by increasing the demand on the storage component of the architecture, whereas it must be abandoned if one puts more realistic constraints on storage" (Baggio, Van Lambalgen, & Hagoort, 2012, p. 18).

The research on ERPs during sentence processing has brought evidence that novel sentences evoke stronger N400 components in the ERP waveform than sentences composed of more expected combinations. The effect reveals a cognitive effort to combine the meaning of a word with the current contextual meaning, suggesting that there is a large amount of stored knowledge in semantic memory about event contingencies and concept combinations, the so-called realistic constraints on storage (Baggio & Hagoort, 2011). In other words: "[compositionality] is no longer a principle applying to language or to linguistic theory as a whole, but a computational constraint on one processing phase . . . in the brain's language system" (Baggio, 2021, p. 15).

In this context, explaining what compositionality is in language should benefit from studies about how systems in the brain realize meaning composition within the bounds of neurophysiological computation. Is the human brain, our computational device, compositional? The challenge is to identify cortical networks and neurophysiological events responsible for composition.

Among others, Hendriks (2020) reviewed the literature about the role of syntax in meaning composition, focusing on children's acquisition of simple transitive sentences such as *The car is pushing the boy.* The major conclusion is that children's *production* of subject–object word order in languages such as English appears to be ahead of their *comprehension* of the subject–object word order. In other words, syntax plays a lesser role (or perhaps a different role) from what is envisaged by the view of syntax–semantics relations in Formal Semantics and generative syntax. Syntactic structure does not fully determine meaning composition. Instead, syntax is merely one of the sources of information constraining meaning and does not have a special status. Conversely, Mollica et al. (2020) investigated how semantic computation can take place when the syntactic structure is not licensed by the language's grammar. The authors introduced a novel manipulation aimed at investigating the neural responses to sentences in which word order is disrupted by increasing the number of local word swaps while maintaining local dependency relationships – that is, combinable words remain close to each other.

(10) a. *She left the museum and walked to her rooms to save money.* (Intact)
 b. *She left the <u>and museum</u> walked to <u>rooms to her</u> save money.* (3swaps)

Using fMRI, they observed that word order degradation did not decrease the magnitude of the blood oxygen level-dependent response in the language network, except when combinable words were put so far apart that the composition among nearby words was doubtful. This observation means that even when the syntactic structure is violated, the language regions respond with equal strength as they did to syntactically correct inputs, confirming that some form of composition still occurs. Given these results, the authors can affirm that "semantic composition," defined as combining the meaning of the words in a sentence without strict syntactic parsing, is the core computation of the language network (Mollica et al., 2020, pp. 125–126).

To conclude, we could argue that compositionality, in the Fregean sense, cannot be considered the core property of natural language. It is still valid that compositional mechanisms exist at the cognitive and brain level, allowing the aggregation of the meaning of expressions. However, compositionality does not exclusively rely on syntactic parsing. In this sense, a reformulation of the classic representation proposed in generative tradition is needed.

5.2 Redefining Compositionality as a Processing Principle

Any model of comprehension aims to explain how language is processed in real time. Specifically, the central question concerns how individuals construct the meaning of a sentence by accessing the meanings of its component lexical items and by integrating those meanings into a coherent configuration.

Two questions are thus the basis of any model of language comprehension: (i) what items are combined, and (ii) how these items are combined and integrated into a final, structured representation. As discussed in Section 2, the strong version of compositionality posits that interpretation is derived from the structure of utterances, with the syntactic form not contributing to semantic information. However, CxG offers a different perspective. First, the semantic primitives of combination are not lexical items, but constructions, that is, form-meaning pairs varying in schematicity and complexity. Some constructions have schematic slots that can be filled with other constructions, which in turn might have slots that can be filled in. Moreover, some constructions are syntactic patterns associated with a specific meaning (e.g., Ditransitive construction), so the interpretation of a sentence is also dependent on syntactic form. In a first, general stance, compositionality in CxG can be defined as follows: "By recognizing the existence of contentful constructions we can save the compositionality in a weakened form: The meaning of an expression is the result of integrating the meaning of the lexical items into the meanings of constructions" (Goldberg, 1995, p. 16).

Therefore, constructions combine freely to form actual expressions as long as they do not conflict (Goldberg, 2003, 2019). For example, a sentence like *Liza sent storage a book* is unacceptable because the ditransitive construction requires an animate recipient argument, while the word *storage* refers to an inanimate argument (Goldberg, 2003, p. 10). This composition is not related to inserting a lexical item into an argument construction, but it can be extended to any construction of different complexity. Grounded on a more formal representation, SBCG (cf. Section 2.2.3) offers a unification-based symbolic formalism for describing the mechanism by which two signs (constructions) are compared to ensure their features do not conflict. If compatible, these signs are merged to form a new, unified sign that combines the attributes and values of the original signs. This unification process operates under constraints specified within the signs themselves, which thus constitute the language grammar. Even though different CxG approaches define the way constructions are combined differently, one thing is clear: Constructions are the rules of compositionality. Syntactic, hierarchical structure with abstract representation does not play a role in comprehension: The specific properties of constructions (which can include surface form constraints as specific word order) are all that matter. In this sense, CxG frameworks adopt a "what you see is what you get" approach (Goldberg, 2003, p. 10).

However, another aspect to consider is that people come to the task of interpretation with a vast amount of shared world knowledge and context (Goldberg, 2015). To this end, the semantic composition is constantly enriched

(Jackendoff, 1997) with background knowledge and contextual constraints: The meaning of a sentence could be computed in a good-enough manner, using expectations instead of building a complete, accurate bottom-up analysis, with the result of leading to shallow interpretation or even misinterpretation (e.g., the renowned Moses illusion, cf. Section 3.2). Models that assume the online processing relies on *chunking* support this hypothesis: Instead of building a syntactic structure serving as support for the comprehension of a sentence, they hypothesize a mechanism that consists of incrementally building chunks at all levels of linguistic structure as rapidly as possible, using all available information predictively to process current input before new information arrives (Blache, 2016; Christiansen & Chater, 2016b, among others). This perspective is shared by usage-based constructionist approaches: "virtually all linguistic expressions, when first constructed, are interpreted with reference to a richly specified situational context, and much of this context is retained as they coalesce to form established units" (Langacker, 1987, p. 455). The notion of compositionality should account for different levels of semantic contribution, from constructional meaning to contextual information and world knowledge. However, most CxG formalisms lack a detailed formalization of how these sources of information are activated and how they contribute to the final interpretation.

A different perspective is offered by Baggio (2021), which tries to include a syntactic form of compositionality. According to his model of language processing, semantic representations may be generated by both a syntax-driven processing stream and an "asyntactic" processing stream, either jointly or independently. Compositionality is viewed as a constraint on computation only in the former stream. This framework, which includes parallel streams for meaning and grammar, embodies these representational and processing capacities, with compositionality serving as a constraint on the syntax-driven stream. When complex natural language expressions have multiple meanings, and at least one of those meanings is solely a function of the meanings of the parts and their syntax, the language system can make predictions about upcoming linguistic inputs based on semantic constraints established by the material already processed. Compositionality is then preserved, but it is considered a specific constraint on computation.

While the centrality of compositionality has been largely minimized, it remains true that human languages possess algorithms for predictably constructing meanings from their parts. However, it is still unclear how the generativity of meaning should be modeled as a computational constraint that influences language processing and its outputs, even though not all complex meanings are equally governed by compositionality (Călinescu, Ramchand, & Baggio, 2023).

5.3 Compositionality, Analogy, and Productivity

Compositionality is often referred to as our ability to compose meanings into endlessly novel configurations. In linguistics, the question of productivity remains a central one: How can a speaker, who has been exposed to a few tons of thousands of sentences, become capable of understanding (and producing) virtually an infinity of utterances?

The previous section introduced the CxG perspective: A speaker interprets a new sentence by relying on the composition of different constructions, which can be defined as "emergent clusters of lossy memory traces that are aligned within our high- (hyper!) dimensional conceptual space on the basis of shared form, function, and contextual dimensions" (Goldberg, 2019, p. 7). Besides, the successful production (or reception) of an utterance depends on previously encountered linguistic expressions, and it is likely to bring up a slight modification to the linguistic knowledge stored in our long-term memory.

> Many approaches to productivity in language assume that computation is called into service in order to avoid storage in memory. That is, it is often assumed that memory and computation stand in an inverse relationship for the sake of efficiency . . . .. The usage-based constructionist approach takes a quite different perspective. Partially abstracted from experience, exemplars are retained in memory as part of a rich network of knowledge. While we are not able to *recall* individual exemplars at will, given that their representations overlap with the representations of other exemplars, our knowledge of language is formed and continually affected by them. Language is extended creatively (involving new "computations"), not in order to reduce or avoid storage in memory, but in order to express new messages in ever-changing contexts. (Goldberg, 2019, p. 134)

This idea of productivity leads to a shift in the linguistic description as well. The mechanism underlying language production is not an a priori set of rules, but it is a force that dynamically changes previous inputs while generating novel outputs. A productive use of a construction is supported to the extent that the potential coinage falls within a densely covered existing cluster of cases that exemplifies the construction. When no conventional constructions are available to express an intended message in context, speakers must extend their existing constructions in novel ways. In the absence of conventional formulations, speakers rely on (combinations of) representations that are sufficiently effective for communication (Goldberg, 2019).

Therefore, the usage-based constructionist perspective allows constructional knowledge to be both remarkably specific and flexible (Goldberg, 2024). According to Goldberg (2019), if a cluster of lossy overlapping memory traces that constitute a construction is very specific, the range of contexts in which it is observed will be narrow. In other words, when observed utterances share similar contexts of use, the resulting learned cluster will be correspondingly narrow and specific. However, even highly specific constructions are occasionally extended flexibly, as speakers must use constructions in constantly changing contexts to convey an open-ended range of messages (Goldberg, 2024).

A tenet of this Element is that a possible mechanism responsible for dealing with extending new constructions is the cognitive process of analogy, the "core of cognition" (Hofstadter, 2001; cf. Section 4.2). Resuming the previously mentioned assumptions of Bybee (2010), analogy depends on similarity in form and meaning between constructions, whether these constructions are of a concrete type (as in collocations or fixed structures) or an abstract type: A novel instance is compared to those stored in our long-term memory to infer the new representation. In this perspective, the probability or acceptability of a novel item is gradient and depends on the extent of similarity to prior uses of a construction. In a more radical stance, Ambridge (2020a) proposed to disregard completely abstraction: Unwitnessed forms are produced and comprehended "by on the fly analogy" across multiple stored exemplars. Similar to what Ambridge (2020a) argued, forms of which one has never had direct experience are produced and understood through "on the fly" analogical processes with respect to multiple stored exemplars (i.e., concrete representations of experiences) and weighed according to their degree of similarity to the new instance; comprehenders generalize via analogy to interpret and generate new linguistic experiences. This mechanism could be applied to entire sentence comprehension: The evolving syntactic structure of the new sentence emerges on the fly as it is compared to the previously interpreted exemplars (Chandler, 2020). In that sense, the mental lexicon could be conceived as a "vast storehouse of triggerable analogies" (Hofstadter, 2001, p. 504): Every lexical expression, when used in speech (whether received or transmitted), could constitute one side of an analogy being made in real time in the speaker's/listener's mind.

However, this assumption does not entirely endorse the radical vision of Ambridge where there is no abstraction: Any kind of analogy is simply untenable without an abstract structure of some sort (Adger, 2020). As already introduced, even constructions are somehow abstracted from their specific instances, and some schemata are more syntactic than concrete expressions.

The hypothesis that analogical mapping with existing, lexicalized construction can be at the basis of productivity does not exclude a priori the existence of other processes that aggregate meaning. Analogy is one possible method of meaning production within a broader array of cognitive mechanisms that not only contribute to productivity but also generate more creative expressions (e.g., *conceptual blending*; cf. Hoffmann, 2024). The central proposal is that productivity is explainable as a continuum: Sometimes, a novel expression can be interpreted analogically from partially overlapping stored sequences, and sometimes, it is the result of a bottom-up compositional computation (defined as unification or other formalisms).

In conclusion, while today's approaches of CxG offer a flexible framework of the construction combinations, more efforts should be made toward a comprehensive description of the mechanisms that undergo three different steps of language (adapted from Kleinschmidt & Jaeger, 2015):

1. How we "recognize the familiar," that is, how we deal with previously experienced and stored aspects of language (lexicalized construction, but also the integration with contextual knowledge);
2. How we "generalize to the similar," that is, how we comprehend a novel situation based on similar previous (linguistic) knowledge to not start from scratch each time a new situation is encountered (productivity); and finally
3. How we "adapt to the novel," that is, how is it possible to adapt beyond what is expected based on previous experience (creativity).

> ### THIS ELEMENT'S CLAIMS ABOUT COMPOSITIONALITY
> **Reduction of the role of Compositionality**
> Compositionality is no longer the undoubted principle applying to language or linguistic theory but a computational constraint on processing in the brain's language system.
> **Productivity is adaptation, and adaptation is by (relational) similarity**
> Comprehension can be viewed as a process of retrieval and adaptation: We interpret linguistic stimuli by recovering the constructions in the semantic memory that best share relational features, and, in case these are not found, we infer (or adapt) the interpretation of the input by analogical inference.

5.4 Toward a Constructionist Model of Language Processing

Defining compositionality is not just a theoretical matter, it is a pressing need for developing a cognitive (and computational) model of language processing. The observations and reviewed literature aim to establish a common ground for designing a formal representation of constructions integrated into a usage-based computational model of language processing – specifically, of language comprehension. Although this is a relatively recent line of research, some works have proposed different hypotheses about bridging the gap between linguistic and psycholinguistic theory (Huettig, Audring, & Jackendoff, 2022; Lindes, 2022; Michel, 2023). An example of frameworks that attempt this integration is presented here.

In terms of representation, Rambelli et al. (2019) provided the formal basis for a constructionist model of language processing. Specifically, they introduced a novel semantic representation of CxG, termed *Distributional Construction Grammar* (DCxG), which integrates constructions with the vector representations used in Distributional Semantics. The primary objectives of this theoretical proposition were twofold: (i) to offer a comprehensive representation of semantic information within the CxG framework, and (ii) to incorporate distributional vectors into the construction representation, thereby accommodating the more usage-based aspects of meaning (Busso, Pannitto, & Lenci, 2018; Lebani & Lenci, 2017; Levshina & Heylen, 2014; Perek, 2016, 2018). Specifically, each construction is represented as an attribute-value matrix following the Signed-Based CxG formalism (Sag et al., 2012). The sources of meaning are encoded separately in three components, which interact but can still be instantiated separately: *constructional meaning, frames*, that is, the schematic knowledge describing scenes and situations in terms of their semantic roles, and *events*, that is, the semantic information concerning particular event instances with their specific participants (McRae & Matsuki, 2009). All these three components are associated with a distributional representation (Figure 4).

Distributional Construction Grammar stands as one of the few works aiming to establish a unified representation of grammar and meaning, grounded on the assumption that language structure and properties emerge from language use. As a linguistic representation, the model develops language structure, properties, and meanings from the distributional statistics observed in text corpora, coherent with the idea that language emerges from language use. On the modeling side, this framework is structured to incorporate linguistic information and world knowledge into the semantic representation of linguistic input, employing an incremental and predictive process. Specifically, this representation has been developed to be the basis of a computational semantic processing model founded on the interaction between the three informational structures with the mechanisms to meaning access: activation, similarity, and unification (Blache et al., 2023).

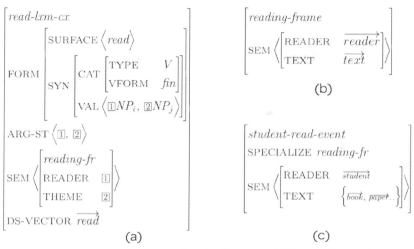

Figure 4 DCxG formalism from Rambelli et al. (2019). (a) The *read* lexeme construction (with its distributional vector), (b) the *reading* frame containing the distributional representation of the semantic roles, and (c) *student-read* event as the specialization of *reading-frame*.

While the previous work is mostly related to a representation aspect, Blache (2024) uses a similar representation to propose a neurocognitive architecture of language processing, integrating constructions and the *Memory, Unification, and Control* model (MUC; cf. Hagoort, 2013, 2016), a general framework for sentence comprehension that aims at accounting for the balance between storage and computation (Baggio, Van Lambalgen, & Hagoort, 2012). Without going into the specific details, this framework relies on two mechanisms: prediction and unification. Prediction calculates the most likely next *sign* (constructions) based on the context. It is always at work and signs (constructions) at any granularity can be predicted. While linguistic theories rely on a mechanism (derivation, constraint solving, etc.) that linearly aggregates objects of categories at the same level, linguistic objects used as basic components can be of any granularity (in line with CxG) and do not necessarily correspond to a category of the same level, meaning that the integration mechanism is no longer linear. Unification, on the other hand, is an operation consisting in comparing two structures, assessing their compatibility, and building a resulting structure merging both. In the case of lexical access, unification is the controlling mechanism for identifying the matching entry. In the case of situation model updating, it implements nonlinear compositionality by integrating the current sign into a structure. This prediction–unification model provides a framework bringing together unique architecture facilitation mechanisms besides classical incremental processing. This is done due to a single processing cycle based on the integration of complex multilevel structures. In addition to explaining how to integrate facilitation mechanisms, this model also brings a new vision about the two different ways to build meaning: compositionality or direct access. In this approach, these two mechanisms only differ in one point: the granularity of the signs to integrate into the situation model. Building the meaning is always done compositionally but can correspond to a word-by-word incremental mechanism (the classical view of compositional principle) or on the opposite in the integration of entire and large pieces of meaning.

The presented models are far from being a complete representation of language processing, and different works could propose different versions of composition (instead of unification) or the alternation of separated cognitive processes, such as analogy, conceptual blending, and so on (Goldberg & Ferreira, 2022; Hoffmann, 2024; Rambelli et al., 2022). In conclusion, new efforts in CxG should be oriented toward integrating construction formalisms into an architecture that combines several processing mechanisms observed in cognitive and neurolinguistic literature. To correctly implement a model of language comprehension, two aspects should be explicitly defined: (i) which type of information resides in the lexicon and in the long-term memory, and how such information is represented, and (ii) which type of principles guide the constraint-based unification that also produces potentially novel combinations. On top of this model, it should be included how the most creative expressions are interpreted (in contrast with productive sentences).

6 Concluding Remarks

This Element has investigated issues at the core foundation of language, issues that are indeed epistemologically complex. The five sections synthesized extensive literature on compositionality and language processing across theoretical, experimental, cognitive, and computational linguistics. On one side, it examined the problem of compositionality, designating both the principle formalized in traditional linguistic theories and the broader cognitive ability observed at the brain level. Conversely, it portrayed a broad scenario in language processing where interpretation is shallow, indeterminate, and often driven by contextual expectations and our preexisting linguistic and world knowledge.

However, the central claim of this Element is that, apart from compositionality, there is another mechanism accounting for language productivity: the cognitive process of analogy. I outlined the key features of analogical reasoning embraced in cognitive studies and explored the nature of linguistic analogy to support the proposal that analogical processing underpins the human capability to create new utterances. Throughout the Element, different observations confirmed the original hypothesis: CxG seems to be the best linguistic theory to characterize the psycholinguistic evidence about language.

While this work aims to converge diverse sources from various domains to present a comprehensive view of the complexity behind language comprehension, there remains a considerable amount of work to integrate these claims into a unified model of language representation and processing. Above all, some aspects of the formalizations proposed in different constructionist approaches still need to be clarified and need future research. According to Kallens and Christiansen (2022, p. 10), a crucial step toward rendering CxG a fully adequate linguistic formalism involves "providing an account of what constructions at different levels of abstraction mean, and how that meaning can be acquired through linguistic experience." Moreover, future efforts should seek to formulate an overarching theory of language comprehension, where input categories of varying granularity (words or constructions) possess a singular representation but engage different mechanisms for accessing meaning (either through composition or direct access).

Another question concerns explicitly the coexistence of these different accesses to meaning and, specifically, the role of analogy. While usage-based theories widely adopt this theoretical concept, there is no work identifying when analogies take place during language comprehension to the best of the author's knowledge. The difficulty lies not only in recognizing the occurrences and their timing but also in the absence of resources enabling a comprehensive study of these phenomena. Consequently, the transition from one mechanism to another remains a challenging question in terms of modeling.

In summary, the primary purpose of this Element is to illustrate what it means to rethink a linguistic theory that considers both traditional compositionality and behavioral observations. Today's challenge is developing linguistic (and computational) models that could address compositional and noncompositional aspects of meaning, using reasonable definitions of compositionality that formally and empirically make the principle nontrivial or nonvacuous. The author hopes that this Element will serve as a valuable resource for students and researchers interested in developing a linguistic architecture capable of modeling the cognitive and linguistic mechanisms involved in sentence interpretation. Future research efforts should move toward delineating a computational model that would integrate formal linguistic theories, usage-based contextual information, and psycholinguistic findings to provide a comprehensive understanding of language comprehension.

References

Abbot-Smith, K., & Tomasello, M. (2006). Exemplar-learning and schematization in a usage-based account of syntactic acquisition. *The Linguistic Review*, *23*(3), 275–290. https://doi.org/10.1515/TLR.2006.011.

Adger, D. (2019). *Language unlimited: The science behind our most creative power*. Oxford: Oxford University Press.

Adger, D. (2020). Syntax and the failure of analogical generalization: A commentary on Ambridge. *First Language*, *40*(5–6), 560–563. https://doi.org/10.1177/0142723720905921.

Albright, A., & Hayes, B. (2003). Rules vs. analogy in English past tenses: A computational/experimental study. *Cognition*, *90*(2), 119–161. https://doi.org/10.1016/S0010-0277(03)00146-X.

Altman, G. T., & Kamide, Y. (1999). Incremental interpretation at verbs: Restricting the domain of subsequent reference. *Cognition*, *73*, 247–264. https://doi.org/10.1016/S0010-0277(99)00059-1.

Ambridge, B. (2010). Children's judgments of regular and irregular novel past-tense forms: New data on the English past-tense debate. *Developmental Psychology*, *46*(6), 1497–1504. https://doi.org/10.1037/a0020668.

Ambridge, B. (2020a). Against stored abstractions: A radical exemplar model of language acquisition. *First Language*, *40*(5–6), 509–559. https://doi.org/10.1177/0142723719869731.

Ambridge, B. (2020b). Abstractions made of exemplars or "You're all right, and I've changed my mind": Response to commentators. *First Language*, *40*(5–6), 640–659. https://doi.org/10.1177/0142723720949723.

Anttila, R. (1977). *Analogy*. The Hague: Mouton.

Arnon, I., & Snider, N. (2010). More than words: Frequency effects for multi-word phrases. *Journal of Memory and Language*, *62*(1), 67–82. https://doi.org/10.1016/j.jml.2009.09.005.

Asher, N. (2015). Types, meanings and coercions in lexical semantics. *Lingua*, *157*, 66–82. https://doi.org/10.1016/j.lingua.2015.01.001.

Asher, N., Van de Cruys, T., Bride, A., & Abrusán, M. (2016). Integrating type theory and distributional semantics: A case study on adjective–noun compositions. *Computational Linguistics*, *42*(4), 703–725. https://doi.org/10.1162/COLI_a_00264.

Baggio, G. (2018). *Meaning in the brain*. Cambridge, MA: MIT Press.

Baggio, G. (2020). Review of M. H. Christiansen & N. Chater, Creating Language: Integrating Evolution, Acquisition, and Processing. *Nordic Journal of Linguistics*, *43*(1), 127–132. doi:10.1017/S0332586519000258.

Baggio, G. (2021). Compositionality in a parallel architecture for language processing. *Cognitive Science*, *45*(5), e12949. https://doi.org/10.1111/cogs .12949.

Baggio, G., & Hagoort, P. (2011). The balance between memory and unification in semantics: A dynamic account of the n400. *Language and Cognitive Processes*, *26*(9), 1338–1367. https://doi.org/10.1080/01690965.2010.542671.

Baggio, G., Van Lambalgen, M., & Hagoort, P. (2012). The processing consequences of compositionality. In W. Hinzen, M. Werning, & E. Machery (Eds.), *The Oxford handbook of compositionality* (pp. 655–672). New York: Oxford University Press. https://doi.org/10.1093/oxfordhb/ 9780199541072.013.0032.

Bannard, C., & Matthews, D. (2008). Stored word sequences in language learning: The effect of familiarity on children's repetition of four-word combinations. *Psychological Science*, *19*(3), 241–248. https://doi.org/ 10.1111/j.1467-9280.2008.02075.x.

Baroni, M., Bernardi, R., & Zamparelli, R. (2014). Frege in space: A program of compositional distributional semantics. *LiLT (Linguistic Issues in Language Technology)*, *9*, 241–346.

Baroni, M., & Zamparelli, R. (2010). Nouns are vectors, adjectives are matrices: Representing adjective-noun constructions in semantic space. In *Proceedings of the 2010 conference on empirical methods in natural language processing* (pp. 1183–1193).

Barton, S. B., & Sanford, A. J. (1993). A case study of anomaly detection: Shallow semantic processing and cohesion establishment. *Memory & Cognition*, *21*(4), 477–487. https://doi.org/10.3758/BF03197179.

Behrens, H. (2017). The role of analogy in language processing and acquisition. In M. Hundt, S. Mollin, & S. E. Pfenninger (Eds.), *The changing English language: Psycholinguistic perspectives* (pp. 215–239). Cambridge: Cambridge University Press.

Beltagy, I., Roller, S., Cheng, P., Erk, K., & Mooney, R. J. (2016). Representing meaning with a combination of logical and distributional mode. *Computational Linguistics*, *42*(4), 763–808. https://doi.org/10.1162/COLI_a_00266.

Bergen, B., & Chang, N. (2005). Embodied construction grammar in simulation-based language understanding. *Construction Grammars: Cognitive Grounding and Theoretical Extensions*, *3*, 147–190. https://doi.org/ 10.1075/cal.3.08ber.

Bergen, B., & Chang, N. (2013). Embodied construction grammar. In T. Hoffmann & G. Trousdale (Eds.), *The Oxford handbook of construction grammar* (pp. 168–190). Oxford: Oxford University Press. https://doi.org/ 10.1093/oxfordhb/9780195396683.013.0010.

Bergs, A. (2018). Learn the rules like a pro, so you can break them like an artist (picasso): Linguistic aberrancy from a constructional perspective. *Zeitschrift für Anglistik und Amerikanistik, 66*(3), 277–293. https://doi.org/10.1515/zaa-2018-0025.

Bergs, A., & Kompa, N. A. (2020). Creativity within and outside the linguistic system. *Cognitive Semiotics, 13*(1), 20202025. https://doi.org/10.1515/cogsem-2020-2025.

Blache, P. (2016). Representing syntax by means of properties: A formal framework for descriptive approaches. *Journal of Language Modelling, 4*(2), 183–224. https://doi.org/10.15398/jlm.v4i2.129.

Blache, P. (2017). Delayed interpretation, shallow processing and constructions: the basis of the "interpret whenever possible" principle. In B. Sharp, F. Sèdes & W. Lubaszewski (Eds.), *Cognitive approach to natural language processing* (pp. 1–19). Oxford: Elsevier. https://doi.org/10.1016/B978-1-78548-253-3.50001-9.

Blache, P. (2024). A neuro-cognitive model of comprehension based on prediction and unification. *Frontiers in Human Neuroscience, 18*, 1356541. https://doi.org/10.3389/fnhum.2024.1356541.

Blache, P., Chersoni, E., Rambelli, G., & Lenci, A. (2023). Composing or Not Composing? Towards Distributional Construction Grammars. (Manuscript submitted for publication)

Blevins, J. P., & Blevins, J. (2009). Introduction: Analogy in grammar. In J. P. Blevins & J. Blevins (Eds.), *Analogy in grammar: Form and acquisition* (pp. 1–12). Oxford: Oxford University Press.

Blumenthal-Dramé, A. (2012). *Entrenchment in usage-based theories*. Berlin: Mouton De Gruyter.

Blything, R. P., Ambridge, B., & Lieven, E. V. (2018). Children's acquisition of the english past-tense: Evidence for a single-route account from novel verb production data. *Cognitive Science, 42*, 621–639. https://doi.org/10.1111/cogs.12581.

Boas, H. C. (2003). *A constructional approach to resultatives*. Stanford: CSLI.

Boas, H. C. (2021). Construction grammar and frame semantics. In John R. Taylor & Wen Xu (Eds.), *The Routledge handbook of cognitive linguistics* (pp. 43–77). New York: Routledge. https://doi.org/10.4324/9781351034708-5.

Bod, R. (2009). From exemplar to grammar: A probabilistic analogy-based model of language learning. *Cognitive Science, 33*(5), 752–793. https://doi.org/10.1111/j.1551-6709.2009.01031.x.

Boleda, G. (2020). Distributional semantics and linguistic theory. *Annual Review of Linguistics*, *6*, 213–234. https://doi.org/10.1146/annurev-linguistics-011619-030303.

Boleda, G., & Herbelot, A. (2016). Formal distributional semantics: Introduction to the special issue. *Computational Linguistics*, *42*(4), 619–635. https://doi.org/10.1162/COLI_a_00261.

Bommasani, R., Hudson, D. A., Adeli, E., et al. (2021). On the opportunities and risks of foundation models. *arXiv preprint arXiv:2108.07258*.

Bos, J., Clark, S., Steedman, M., Curran, J. R., & Hockenmaier, J. (2004). Wide-coverage semantic representations from a ccg parser. In *COLING 2004: Proceedings of the 20th international conference on computational linguistics* (pp. 1240–1246).

Boyland, J. T. (2009). Usage-based models of language. In D. Eddington (Ed.), *Experimental and quantitative linguistics* (pp. 351–419). Munich: Lincom.

Busso, L., Pannitto, L., & Lenci, A. (2018). Modelling Italian Construction Flexibility with Distributional Semantics: Are Constructions Enough? In *Proceedings of the fifth Italian conference on computational linguistics (clic-it 2018)* (pp. 68–74). https://doi.org/10.4000/books.aaccademia.310.

Bybee, J. L. (2006). From usage to grammar: The mind's response to repetition. *Language*, *82*(4), 711–733. https://muse.jhu.edu/article/208049.

Bybee, J. L. (2010). *Language, usage and cognition*. Cambridge: Cambridge University Press.

Bybee, J. L., & Moder, C. L. (1983). Morphological classes as natural categories. *Language*, *59*(2), 251–270. https://doi.org/10.2307/413574.

Cacciari, C., Corrardini, P., & Ferlazzo, F. (2018). Cognitive and personality components underlying spoken idiom comprehension in context. An exploratory study. *Frontiers in Psychology*, *9*, 659. https://doi.org/10.3389/fpsyg.2018.00659.

Cacciari, C., & Tabossi, P. (1988). The comprehension of idioms. *Journal of Memory and Language*, *27*(6), 668–683. https://doi.org/10.1016/0749-596X(88)90014-9.

Călinescu, L., Ramchand, G., & Baggio, G. (2023). How (not) to look for meaning composition in the brain: A reassessment of current experimental paradigms. *Frontiers in Language Sciences*, *2*, 1096110. https://doi.org/10.3389/flang.2023.1096110.

Carrol, G., & Conklin, K. (2020). Is all formulaic language created equal? unpacking the processing advantage for different types of formulaic sequences. *Language and Speech*, *63*(1), 95–122. https://doi.org/10.1177/0023830918823230.

Chandler, S. (2017). The analogical modeling of linguistic categories. *Language and Cognition: An Interdisciplinary Journal of Language and Cognitive Science, 9*(1), 52–87. https://psycnet.apa.org/doi/10.1017/langcog.2015.24.

Chandler, S. (2020). Sentence-level constructions: A demonstration in support of Ambridge. *First Language, 40*(5–6), 569–572. https://doi.org/10.1177/0142723720905764.

Chaves, R. P. (2019). Construction grammar. In A. Kertész, E. Moravcsik, & C. Rákosi (Eds.), *Current approaches to syntax. A comparative handbook* (pp. 49–96). Berlin: Mouton De Gruyter. https://doi.org/10.1515/9783110540253-003.

Chomsky, N. (1957). *Syntactic structures*. The Hague: Mouton.

Chomsky, N. (1965). *Aspects of the theory of syntax*. Cambridge, MA: MIT Press.

Christiansen, M. H., & Chater, N. (2016a). *Creating language: Integrating evolution, acquisition, and processing*. Cambridge, MA: MIT Press.

Christiansen, M. H., & Chater, N. (2016b). The Now-or-Never bottleneck: A fundamental constraint on language. *Behavioral Brain Science, 39*, e39–e62. https://doi.org/10.1017/S0140525X1500031X.

Christianson, K., Hollingworth, A., Halliwell, J. F., & Ferreira, F. (2001). Thematic roles assigned along the garden path linger. *Cognitive Psychology, 42*(4), 368–407. https://doi.org/10.1006/cogp.2001.0752.

Coecke, B., Sadrzadeh, M., & Clark, S. (2010). Mathematical foundations for a compositional distributional model of meaning. *ArXiv, abs/1003.4394*.

Colmerauer, A. (1982). An interesting subset of natural language. In K. Clark & S. Tärnlund (Eds.), *Logic programming* (pp. 45–66). Orlando, FL: Academic Press.

Contreras Kallens, P., & Christiansen, M. H. (2022). Models of language and multiword expressions. *Frontiers Artificial Intelligence Appl., 5*, 43–77. https://doi.org/10.3389/frai.2022.781962.

Coolen, R., Van Jaarsveld, H. J., & Schreuder, R. (1991). The interpretation of isolated novel nominal compounds. *Memory & Cognition, 19*, 341–352. https://doi.org/10.3758/BF03197138.

Copestake, A., Flickinger, D., Pollard, C., & Sag, I. A. (2005). Minimal recursion semantics: An introduction. *Research on Language and Computation, 3*(2), 281–332. https://doi.org/10.1007/s11168-006-6327-9.

Croft, W. (1991). *Syntactic categories and grammatical relations: The cognitive organization of information*. Chicago: University of Chicago Press.

Croft, W. (2001). *Radical construction grammar: Syntactic theory in typological perspective*. Oxford: Oxford University Press. https://doi.org/10.1093/acprof:oso/9780198299554.001.0001.

Croft, W., & Cruse, D. A. (2004). *Cognitive linguistics*. Cambridge: Cambridge University Press. https://doi.org/10.1017/CBO9780511803864.

Culicover, P. W., & Jackendoff, R. (1999). The view from the periphery: The English comparative correlative. *Linguistic Inquiry*, *30*(4), 543–571. https://doi.org/10.1093/acprof:oso/9780199271092.003.0014.

Culicover, P. W., & Jackendoff, R. (2006). The simpler syntax hypothesis. *Trends in Cognitive Sciences*, *10*(9), 413–418. https://doi.org/10.1016/j.tics.2006.07.007.

Dąbrowska, E. (2017). *Ten lectures on grammar in the mind*. Leiden: Brill.

Daelemans, W., & Van Den Bosch, A. (2010). Memory-based learning. *The Handbook of Computational Linguistics and Natural Language Processing*, 154–179.

DeLong, K. A., Urbach, T. P., & Kutas, M. (2005). Probabilistic word pre-activation during language comprehension inferred from electrical brain activity. *Nature Neuroscience*, *8*, 1117–1121. https://doi.org/10.1038/nn1504.

Del Pinal, G. (2015). *The semantic architecture of the faculty of language: compositional operations and complex lexical representations* (Unpublished doctoral dissertation). Columbia University, New York, NY.

Diessel, H. (2019). *The grammar network: How linguistic structure is shaped by language use*. Cambridge: Cambridge University Press.

Diessel, H. (2023). *The constructicon: Taxonomies and networks*. Cambridge: Cambridge University Press.

Dowty, D. (2007). Compositionality as an empirical problem. In C. Barker & P. I. Jacobson (Eds.), *Direct compositionality* (pp. 14–23). Oxford: Oxford University Press. https://doi.org/10.1093/oso/9780199204373.003.0002.

Elman, J. L. (2009). On the meaning of words and dinosaur bones: Lexical knowledge without a lexicon. *Cognitive Science*, *33*(4), 547–582. https://doi.org/10.1111/j.1551-6709.2009.01023.x.

Elman, J. L. (2011). Lexical knowledge without a lexicon? *The Mental Lexicon*, *6*, 1–33. https://doi.org/10.1075/ml.6.1.01elm.

Elman, J. L. (2014). Systematicity in the lexicon: On having your cake and eating it too. In P. Calvo & J. Symons (Eds.), *The architecture of cognition* (pp. 115–145). Cambridge, MA: The MIT Press. https://doi.org/10.7551/mitpress/9559.003.0008.

Erickson, T. D., & Mattson, M. E. (1981). From words to meaning: A semantic illusion. *Journal of Verbal Learning and Verbal Behavior*, *20*(5), 540–551. https://doi.org/10.1016/S0022-5371(81)90165-1.

Erk, K., & Padó, S. (2008). A structured vector space model for word meaning in context. In *Proceedings of the conference on empirical methods in natural language processing* (pp. 897–906).

Falkenhainer, B., Forbus, K. D., & Gentner, D. (1989). The structure-mapping engine: Algorithm and examples. *Artificial Intelligence*, *41*(1), 1–63. https://doi.org/10.1016/0004-3702(89)90077-5.

Fauconnier, G., & Turner, M. (2002). *The way we think: Conceptual blending and the mind's hidden complexities*. New York: Basic books.

Ferreira, F. (2003). The misinterpretation of noncanonical sentences. *Cognitive Psychology*, *47*(2), 164–203. https://doi.org/10.1016/S0010-0285(03)00005-7.

Ferreira, F., Bailey, K. G., & Ferraro, V. (2002). Good-enough representations in language comprehension. *Current Directions in Psychological Science*, *11*(1), 11–15. https://doi.org/10.1111/1467-8721.00158.

Ferreira, F., Christianson, K., & Hollingworth, A. (2001). Misinterpretations of garden-path sentences: Implications for models of sentence processing and reanalysis. *Journal of Psycholinguistic Research*, *30*(1), 3–20. https://doi.org/10.1023/A:1005290706460.

Ferreira, F., & Lowder, M. W. (2016). Prediction, information structure, and good-enough language processing. In B. H. Ross (Ed.), *Psychology of Learning and Motivation* (Vol. 65, pp. 217–247). San Diego: Academic Press. https://doi.org/10.1016/bs.plm.2016.04.002.

Ferreira, F., & Patson, N. D. (2007). The "good enough" approach to language comprehension. *Language and Linguistics Compass*, *1*(1–2), 71–83. https://doi.org/10.1111/j.1749-818X.2007.00007.x.

Ferretti, T. R., McRae, K., & Hatherell, A. (2001). Integrating verbs, situation schemas, and thematic role concepts. *Journal of Memory and Language*, *44*(4), 516–547. https://doi.org/10.1006/jmla.2000.2728.

Fillmore, C. J. (1982). Frame semantics. In The Linguistic Society of Korea (Ed.), (pp. 111–137). Seoul: Hanshin Pub. Co.

Fillmore, C. J., & Baker, C. (2010). A frames approach to semantic analysis. In Bernd Heine & Heiko Narrog (Eds.), *The Oxford handbook of linguistic analysis* (pp. 313–340). Oxford: Oxford University Press.

Fillmore, C. J., Kay, P., & O'Connor, M. C. (1988). Regularity and idiomaticity in grammatical constructions: The case of let alone. *Language*, *64*(3), 501–138. https://doi.org/10.2307/414531.

Firth, J. R. (1957). A synopsis of linguistic theory, 1930–1955. In J. R. Firth (Ed.), *Studies in linguistic analysis* (pp. 1–31). Special Volume of the Philological Society. Oxford: Blackwell.

Fodor, J. A. (2001). Language, thought and compositionality. *Royal Institute of Philosophy Supplements*, *48*, 227–242. https://doi.org/10.1017/S1358246100010808.

Fodor, J. A., & Pylyshyn, Z. W. (1988). Connectionism and cognitive architecture: A critical analysis. *Cognition*, *28*(1–2), 3–71. https://doi.org/10.1016/0010-0277(88)90031-5.

Forbus, K. D., Ferguson, R. W., Lovett, A., & Gentner, D. (2017). Extending sme to handle large-scale cognitive modeling. *Cognitive Science*, *41*(5), 1152–1201. https://doi.org/10.1111/cogs.12377.

Gagné, C. L. (2001). Relation and lexical priming during the interpretation of noun–noun combinations. *Journal of Experimental Psychology: Learning, Memory, and Cognition*, *27*(1), 236–254. https://doi.org/10.1037//0278-7393.27.1.236.

Gagné, C. L., & Shoben, E. J. (1997). Influence of thematic relations on the comprehension of modifier–noun combinations. *Journal of Experimental Psychology: Learning, Memory, and Cognition*, *23*(1), 71–87. https://psycnet.apa.org/doi/10.1037/0278-7393.23.1.71.

Garrette, D., Erk, K., & Mooney, R. (2014). A formal approach to linking logical form and vector-space lexical semantics. In H. Bunt, J. Bos, & S. Pulman (Eds.), *Computing meaning. Text, speech and language technology* (Vol 47). Springer, Dordrecht. https://doi.org/10.1007/978-94-007-7284-7_3.

Gayral, F., Kayser, D., & Lévy, F. (2005). Challenging the principle of compositionality in interpreting natural language texts. In E. Machery, M. Werning, & G. Schurz (Eds.), *The compositionality of meaning and content*, Vol. 2 in the series Linguistics & Philosophy (pp. 83–106). Heusenstamm: Ontos Verlang. https://doi.org/10.1515/9783110332865.83.

Gentner, D. (1983). Structure-mapping: A theoretical framework for analogy. *Cognitive Science*, *7*(2), 155–170. https://doi.org/10.1016/S0364-0213(83)80009-3.

Gentner, D. (1988). Metaphor as structure mapping: The relational shift. *Child Development*, *59*, 47–59. https://psycnet.apa.org/doi/10.2307/1130388.

Gentner, D., & Markman, A. B. (1997). Structure mapping in analogy and similarity. *American Psychologist*, *52*(1), 45–56. https://psycnet.apa.org/doi/10.1037/0003-066X.52.1.45.

Gentner, D., & Smith, L. A. (2012). Analogical reasoning. In V. S. Ramachandran (Ed.), *Encyclopedia of human behavior* (2nd ed.) (pp. 130–136). Oxford: Elsevier. https://doi.org/10.1016/B978-0-12-375000-6.00022-7.

Gentner, D., & Smith, L. A. (2013). Analogical learning and reasoning. In *The Oxford handbook of cognitive psychology* (pp. 668–681). New York: Oxford University Press. https://doi.org/10.1093/oxfordhb/9780195376746.013.0042.

Gibbs, R. W. (1980). Spilling the beans on understanding and memory for idioms in conversation. *Memory & Cognition, 8*(2), 149–156. https://doi.org/10.3758/BF03213418.

Gibbs, R. W., Nayak, N. P., & Cutting, C. (1989). How to kick the bucket and not decompose: Analyzability and idiom processing. *Journal of Memory and Language, 28*(5), 576–593. https://doi.org/10.1016/0749-596X(89)90014-4.

Giora, R., Fein, O., Kronrod, A., et al. (2004). Weapons of mass distraction: Optimal innovation and pleasure ratings. *Metaphor and Symbol, 19*(2), 115–141. https://doi.org/10.1207/s15327868ms1902_2.

Goldberg, A. E. (1995). *Constructions: A construction grammar approach to argument structure.* Chicago: University of Chicago Press.

Goldberg, A. E. (2003). Constructions: A new theoretical approach to language. *Trends in Cognitive Sciences, 7*(5), 219–224. https://doi.org/10.1016/S1364-6613(03)00080-9.

Goldberg, A. E. (2006). *Constructions at work: The nature of generalization in language.* New York: Oxford University Press.

Goldberg, A. E. (2013). Constructionist approaches. In Thomas Hoffmann & Graeme Trousdale (Eds), *The Oxford handbook of construction grammar* (pp. 14–31). Oxford: Oxford University Press.

Goldberg, A. E. (2015). Compositionality. In N. Riemer (Ed.), *The Routledge handbook of semantics* (pp. 435–449). New York: Routledge.

Goldberg, A. E. (2019). *Explain me this: Creativity, competition, and the partial productivity of constructions.* Princeton: Princeton University Press.

Goldberg, A. E. (2024). A chat about constructionist approaches and llms. *Constructions and Frames, special issue.* (to appear). https://doi.org/10.31234/osf.io/8bmwz.

Goldberg, A. E., & Ferreira, F. (2022). Good-enough language production. *Trends in Cognitive Sciences, 26*(4), 300–311. https://doi.org/10.1016/j.tics.2022.01.005.

Goldberg, A. E., & Jackendoff, R. (2004). The english resultative as a family of constructions. *Language, 80*, 532–568. https://doi.org/10.1353/LAN.2004.0129.

Groenendijk, J., & Stokhof, M. (2005). Why compositionality. In G. N. Carlson & F. J. Pelletier (Eds.), *Reference and quantification: The partee effect* (pp. 83–106). Stanford: CSLI.

Gulordava, K., Bojanowski, P., Grave, E., Linzen, T., & Baroni, M. (2018, June). Colorless green recurrent networks dream hierarchically. In M. Walker, H. Ji, & A. Stent (Eds.), *Proceedings of the 2018 conference of the North American chapter of the association for computational linguistics: Human language technologies, volume 1 (long papers)* (pp. 1195–1205). New Orleans, Louisiana: Association for Computational Linguistics. https://doi.org/10.18653/v1/N18-1108.

Hagoort, P. (2013). MUC (Memory, Unification, Control) and beyond. *Frontiers in Psychology*, *4*, 1–13. https://doi.org/10.33892Ffpsyg.2013.00416.

Hagoort, P. (2016). MUC (Memory, Unification, Control): A model on the neurobiology of language beyond single word processing. In G. Hickok & S. L. Small (Eds.), *Neurobiology of language* (pp. 339–347). San Diego: Elsevier. https://doi.org/10.1016/B978-0-12-407794-2.00028-6.

Hagoort, P., Baggio, G., & Willems, R. M. (2009). Semantic unification. *The Cognitive Neurosciences*, 819–836. https://psycnet.apa.org/doi/10.7551/mitpress/8029.003.0072.

Hale, J. (2001). A probabilistic earley parser as a psycholinguistic model. In *Proceedings of the second meeting of the North American chapter of the association for computational linguistics on language technologies* (p. 1–8). USA: Association for Computational Linguistics. 10.3115/1073336.1073357.

Harris, Z. S. (1954). Distributional structure. *Word*, *10*, 146–162. https://doi.org/10.1080/00437956.1954.11659520.

Hartmann, S., & Ungerer, T. (2023). Attack of the snowclones: A corpus-based analysis of extravagant formulaic patterns. *Journal of Linguistics*, 1–36. https://doi.org/10.1017/S0022226723000117.

Haspelmath, M. (1999). Why is grammaticalization irreversible? *Linguistics*, *37*, 1043–1068. https://doi.org/10.1515/ling.37.6.1043.

Hauser, M. D., Chomsky, N., & Fitch, W. T. (2002). The faculty of language: What is it, who has it, and how did it evolve? *Science*, *298*(5598), 1569–1579. https://doi.org/10.1126/science.298.5598.1569.

Hendriks, P. (2020). The acquisition of compositional meaning. *Philosophical Transactions of the Royal Society B*, *375*(1791), 20190312.

Hilpert, M. (2019). *Construction grammar and its application to English* (2 ed.). Edinburgh: Edinburgh University Press.

Hilpert, M. (2021). *Ten lectures on diachronic construction grammar*. Leiden: Brill.

Hinzen, W., Werning, M., & Machery, E. (2012a). Introduction. In W. Hinzen, M. Werning, & E. Machery (Eds.), *The Oxford handbook of compositionality* (pp. 1–16). New York: Oxford University Press.

Hinzen, W., Werning, M., & Machery, E. (Eds.). (2012b). *The Oxford handbook of compositionality*. New York: Oxford University Press.

Hock, H. H. (2003). Analogical change. In Brain D. Joseph & Richard D. Janda (Eds.), *The handbook of historical linguistics* (pp. 441–460). Oxford: Blackwell.

Hoffmann, T. (2017). Construction grammars. In B. Dancygier (Ed.), *The Cambridge handbook of cognitive linguistics* (pp. 310–329). Cambridge: Cambridge University Press. https://doi.org/10.1017/9781316339732.020.

Hoffmann, T. (2018). Creativity and construction grammar: Cognitive and psychological issues. *Zeitschrift für Anglistik und Amerikanistik, 66*(3), 259–276. https:doi.org/10.1515/zaa-2018-0024.

Hoffmann, T. (2019). Language and creativity: A construction grammar approach to linguistic creativity. *Linguistics Vanguard, 5*(1), 20190019. https://doi.org/10.1515/lingvan-2019-0019.

Hoffmann, T. (2022a). *Construction grammar*. Cambridge: Cambridge University Press.

Hoffmann, T. (2022b). *Construction grammar: The structure of English*. Cambridge: Cambridge University Press.

Hoffmann, T. (2024). Cognitive approaches to linguistic creativity. To appear in: The Cambridge Encyclopedia of Cognitive Linguistics. doi:10.33774/coe-2024-8tnps

Hoffman, T., & Bergs, A. (2018). A construction grammar approach to genre. *CogniTextes. Revue de l'Association française de linguistique cognitive* (Volume 18). https://doi.org/10.4000/cognitextes.1032.

Hoffmann, T., Brunner, T., & Horsch, J. (2020). English comparative correlative constructions: A usage-based account. *Open Linguistics*, 196–215. https://doi.org/10.1515/opli-2020-0012.

Hoffmann, T., & Trousdale, G. (Eds.). (2013). *The Oxford handbook of construction grammar*. Oxford: Oxford University Press.

Hofstadter, D. R. (1985). Analogies and role in human and machine thinking. In D. R. Hofstadter (Ed.), *Metamagical themas: Questing for the essence of mind and pattern* (Ch. 24, pp. 547–603). New York: Basic Books, Inc.

Hofstadter, D. R. (2001). Analogy as the core of cognition. In K. J. Holyoak, D. Gentner, & B. N. Kokinov (Eds.), *The analogical mind: Perspectives from cognitive science* (pp. 499–538). Cambridge, MA: The MIT Press.

Hofstadter, D. R. (2009). *Analogy as the core of cognition.* www.youtube.com/watch?v=n8m7lFQ3njk.

Hofstadter, D. R., & Mitchell, M. (1994). The copycat project: A model of mental fluidity and analogy-making. In K. J. Holyoak & J. A. Barnden (Eds.), *Analogical connections* (pp. 31–112). New York: Ablex.

Holyoak, K. J. (2012). Analogy and relational reasoning. *The Oxford Handbook of Thinking and Reasoning, 836*, 234–259.

Holyoak, K. J., Gentner, D., & Kokinov, B. N. (2001). The place of analogy in cognition. In K. J. Holyoak, D. Gentner, & B. N. Kokinov (Eds.), *The analogical mind: Perspectives from cognitive science* (pp. 1–19). Cambridge, MA: MIT Press.

Huettig, F. (2015). Four central questions about prediction in language processing. *Brain Research, 1626*, 118–135. https://doi.org/10.1016/j.brainres.2015.02.014.

Huettig, F., Audring, J., & Jackendoff, R. (2022). A parallel architecture perspective on pre-activation and prediction in language processing. *Cognition, 224*, 105050. https://doi.org/10.1016/j.cognition.2022.105050.

Hupkes, D., Dankers, V., Mul, M., & Bruni, E. (2020). Compositionality decomposed: How do neural networks generalise? *Journal of Artificial Intelligence Research, 67*, 757–795.

Ibbotson, P. (2013). The scope of usage-based theory. *Frontiers in Psychology, 4*, 1–15.

Ichien, N., Liu, Q., Fu, S., et al. (2021). Visual analogy: Deep learning versus compositional models. In *Proceedings of the 43rd annual meeting of the cognitive science society.* Cognitive Science Society.

Jackendoff, R. (1997). *The architecture of the language faculty* (No. 28). Cambridge, MA: MIT Press.

Jackendoff, R. (2002). *Foundations of language: Brain, meaning, grammar, evolution.* New York: Oxford University Press.

Jackendoff, R. (2013). Constructions in the parallel architecture. In T. Hoffmann & G. Trousdale (Eds.), *The Oxford handbook of construction grammar* (pp. 70–92). Oxford: Oxford University Press. https://doi.org/10.1093/oxfordhb/9780195396683.013.0005.

Jakubíček, M., Kilgarriff, A., Kovář, V., Rychlý, P., & Suchomel, V. (2013). The tenten corpus family. In *7th international corpus linguistics conference cl* (pp. 125–127).

Janssen, T. M., & Partee, B. H. (1997). Compositionality. In Johan van Benthem & Alice ter Meulen (Eds.), *Handbook of logic and language* (pp. 417–473). Amsterdam: Elsevier.

Jiang, S., Jiang, X., & Siyanova-Chanturia, A. (2020). The processing of multiword expressions in children and adults: An eye-tracking study of Chinese. *Applied Psycholinguistics, 41*(4), 901–931.

Johns, B. T., & Jones, M. N. (2015). Generating structure from experience: A retrieval-based model of language processing. *Canadian Journal of Experimental Psychology, 69*(3), 233–251.

Jolsvai, H., McCauley, S. M., & Christiansen, M. H. (2020). Meaningfulness beats frequency in multiword chunk processing. *Cognitive Science, 44*(10), e12885.

Kamp, H., & Reyle, U. (1993). *From discourse to logic: Introduction to modeltheoretic semantics of natural language, formal logic and discourse representation theory*. Dordrecht: Kluwer Academic Publishers.

Kaplan, A. (2017). Exemplar-based models in linguistics *obo* in Linguistics. doi: 10.1093/obo/9780199772810-0201

Kay, P., & Michaelis, L. A. (2012). Constructional meaning and compositionality. *Semantics: An International Handbook of Natural Language Meaning, 3*, 2271–2296.

Kim, A., & Osterhout, L. (2005). The independence of combinatory semantic processing: Evidence from event-related potentials. *Journal of Memory and Language, 52*(2), 205–225.

King, J. C. (2006). Formal semantics. In B. C. Smith (Ed.), *The Oxford handbook of philosophy of language* (pp. 557–573). Oxford: Oxford University Press.

Kleinschmidt, D. F., & Jaeger, T. F. (2015). Robust speech perception: Recognize the familiar, generalize to the similar, and adapt to the novel. *Psychological Review, 122*(2), 148–203. https://doi.org/10.1037/a0038695.

Krott, A. (2009). 1186 The role of analogy for compound words. In James P. Blevins & Juliette Blevins (Eds.), *Analogy in grammar: Form and acquisition* (pp. 18–136). Oxford: Oxford University Press. https://doi.org/10.1093/acprof:oso/9780199547548.003.0006.

Kuperberg, G. R., & Jaeger, T. F. (2015). What do we mean by prediction in language comprehension? *Language Cognition & Neuroscience, 3798*, 32–59.

Lake, B., & Baroni, M. (2018). Generalization without systematicity: On the compositional skills of sequence-to-sequence recurrent networks. In J. Dy & A. Krause (Eds.), *35th International Conference on Machine Learning, ICML 2018* (Vol. 7, pp. 4487–4499). International Machine Learning Society (IMLS).

Langacker, R. W. (1987). *Foundations of cognitive grammar: Theoretical prerequisites* (Vol. 1). Stanford: Stanford University Press.

Langacker, R. W. (1999). Grammar and Conceptualization. Berlin and New York: De Gruyter Mouton. https://doi.org/10.1515/9783110800524.

Lebani, G. E., & Lenci, A. (2017). Modelling the Meaning of Argument Constructions with Distributional Semantics. In *Proceedings of the AAAI 2017 spring symposium on computational construction grammar and natural language understanding* (pp. 197–204).

Leech, G. N. (2014). *A linguistic guide to English poetry*. New York: Routledge.

Lenci, A. (2018). Distributional models of word meaning. *Annual Review of Linguistics, 4*(1), 151–171.

Lenci, A., & Sahlgren, M. (2023). *Distributional semantics*. Cambridge: Cambridge University Press. https://doi.org/10.1017/9780511783692.

Levin, B., & Hovav, M. R. (1995). *Unaccusativity: At the syntax-lexical semantics interface* (Vol. 26). Cambridge, MA: MIT press.

Levshina, N., & Heylen, K. (2014). A radically data-driven construction grammar: Experiments with Dutch causative constructions. In Ronny Boogaart, Timothy Colleman, & Gijsbert Rutten (Eds.), *Extending the scope of construction grammar* (pp. 17–46). Berlin: Mouton de Gruyter.

Levy, R. (2008). Expectation-based Syntactic Comprehension. *Cognition, 106*(3), 1126–1177.

Levy, O., & Goldberg, Y. (2014). Dependency-based word embeddings. In *Proceedings of the 52nd annual meeting of the association for computational linguistics (volume 2: Short papers)*. Stroudsburg, PA, USA: Association for Computational Linguistics.

Libben, G. (2014). The nature of compounds: A psychocentric perspective. *Cognitive Neuropsychology, 31*(1–2), 8–25.

Libben, M., & Titone, D. (2008). The multidetermined nature of idiom processing. *Memory & Cognition, 36*(6), 1103–1121.

Lindes, P. (2022). *Constructing meaning, piece by piece: A computational cognitive model of human sentence comprehension* (Doctoral dissertation University of Michigan, nn Arbor, MI). https://dx.doi.org/10.7302/4697.

Linzen, T., Dupoux, E., & Goldberg, Y. (2016). Assessing the ability of lstms to learn syntax-sensitive dependencies. *Transactions of the Association for Computational Linguistics, 4*, 521–535.

Loula, J., Baroni, M., & Lake, B. M. (2018). Rearranging the familiar: Testing compositional generalization in recurrent networks. *arXiv preprint arXiv:1807.07545*.

Maienborn, C., von Heusinger, K., & Portner, P. (2011). *Semantics: An international handbook of natural language meaning* (Vol. 1). Berlin: Walter de Gruyter.

Martin, A. E., & Baggio, G. (2020). Modelling meaning composition from formalism to mechanism. *Philosophical Transactions of the Royal Society B, 375*(1791), 20190298. https://doi.org/10.1098/rstb.2019.0298.

Mattiello, E. (2016). Analogical neologisms in English. *Italian Journal of Linguistics*, *28*(2), 103–142.

Mattiello, E. (2017). *Analogy in word-formation: A study of English neologisms and occasionalisms* (Vol. 309). Berlin: Walter de Gruyter.

Maybin, J. (2015). Everyday language creativity. In Rodney Jones (ed.), *The Routledge handbook of language and creativity* (pp. 25–39). New York: Routledge.

McCauley, S. M., & Christiansen, M. H. (2019). Language learning as language use: A cross-linguistic model of child language development. *Psychological Review*, *126*(1), 1–51.

McRae, K., Hare, M., Elman, J. L., & Ferretti, T. (2005). A basis for generating expectancies for verbs from nouns. *Memory & Cognition*, *33*(7), 1174–1184.

McRae, K., & Matsuki, K. (2009). People use their knowledge of common events to understand language, and do so as quickly as possible. *Language and Linguistics Compass*, *3*(6), 1417–1429.

McRae, K., Spivey-Knowlton, M. J., & Tanenhaus, M. K. (1998). Modeling the influence of thematic fit (and other constraints) in on line sentence comprehension. *Journal of Memory and Language*, *38*(3), 283–312.

Metusalem, R., Kutas, M., Urbach, T. P., et al. (2012). Generalized event knowledge activation during online sentence comprehension. *Journal of Memory and Language*, *66*(4), 545–567.

Michaelis, L. A. (2013). Sign-based construction grammar. In T. Hoffmann & G. Trousdale (Eds.), *The Oxford handbook of construction grammar* (pp. 133–152). Oxford: Oxford University Press.

Michaelis, L. A. (2015). 147Sign-based construction grammar. In Bernd Heine & Heiko Narrog (Eds.), *The Oxford handbook of linguistic analysis* (pp. 139–158) Oxford: Oxford University Press. https://doi.org/10.1093/oxfordhb/9780199677078.013.0007.

Michaelis, L. A. (in press). Meaning and sign based construction grammar. In C. Sinha & X. Wen (Eds.), *Cambridge encyclopedia of cognitive linguistics.* Cambridge: Cambridge University Press.

Michel, C. (2023). Scaling up predictive processing to language with construction grammar. *Philosophical Psychology*, *36*(3), 553–579. https://doi.org/10.1080/09515089.2022.2050198.

Mikolov, T., Yih, W.- t., & Zweig, G. (2013). Linguistic regularities in continuous space word representations. In *Proceedings of the 2013 conference of the North American chapter of the association for computational linguistics: Human language technologies* (pp. 746–751).

Miller, G. A., & Charles, W. G. (1991). Contextual correlates of semantic similarity. *Language and Cognitive Processes*, *6*(1), 1–28.

Mitchell, M. (2021). Abstraction and analogy-making in artificial intelligence. *Annals of the New York Academy of Sciences, 1505*(1), 79–101.

Mitchell, J., & Lapata, M. (2008). Vector-based models of semantic composition. In *proceedings of acl-08: Hlt* (pp. 236–244).

Mitchell, J., & Lapata, M. (2010). Composition in distributional models of semantics. *Cognitive Science, 34*(8), 1388–1429. https://doi.org/10.1111/j.1551-6709.2010.01106.x.

Mitchell, J., Lapata, M., Demberg, V., & Keller, F. (2010). Syntactic and Semantic Factors in Processing Difficulty: An Integrated Measure. In *Proceedings of ACL* (pp. 196–206). Uppsala, Sweden.

Molinaro, N., & Carreiras, M. (2010). Electrophysiological evidence of interaction between contextual expectation and semantic integration during the processing of collocations. *Biological Psychology, 83*(3), 176–190.

Mollica, F., Siegelman, M., Diachek, E., et al. (2020). Composition is the core driver of the language-selective network. *Neurobiology of Language, 1*(1), 104–134.

Montague, R. (1970a). English as a formal language. In B. Visentini (Ed.), *Linguaggi nella societa e nella tecnica* (pp. 188–221). Bologna: Edizioni di Communita.

Montague, R. (1970b). Universal grammar. *Theoria, 36*(3), 373–398.

Montague, R. (1973). The proper treatment of quantification in ordinary English. In K. Hintikka, E. Moravcsik, & P. Suppes (Eds.), *Approaches to natural language* (pp. 221–242). Dordrecht: Springer.

Moot, R. (2012). Wide-coverage semantics for spatio-temporal reasoning. *Trait. Autom. des Langues, 53*(2), 115–142.

Nosofsky, R. M. (1990). Relations between exemplar-similarity and likelihood models of classification. *Journal of Mathematical Psychology, 34*(4), 393–418.

Paczynski, M., & Kuperberg, G. R. (2012). Multiple influences of semantic memory on sentence processing: Distinct effects of semantic relatedness on violations of real-world event/state knowledge and animacy selection restrictions. *Journal of Memory and Language, 67*(4), 426–448.

Pagin, P., & Westerståhl, D. (2010a). Compositionality i: Definitions and variants. *Philosophy Compass, 5*(3), 250–264.

Pagin, P., & Westerståhl, D. (2010b). Compositionality ii: Arguments and problems. *Philosophy Compass, 5*(3), 265–282.

Paperno, D., Pham, N. T., & Baroni, M. (2014). A practical and linguistically-motivated approach to compositional distributional semantics. In *Proceedings of the 52nd annual meeting of the association for computational linguistics (volume 1: Long papers)* (pp. 90–99).

Partee, B. H. (1995). Lexical semantics and compositionality. In L. Gleitman & M. Liberman (Eds.), *Language: An invitation to cognitive science* (pp. 311–360). Cambridge, MA: The MIT Press.

Partee, B. H. (2004). *Compositionality in formal semantics: Selected papers.* Oxford: Blackwell.

Partee, B. H. (2016). Formal semantics. In M. Aloni & P. Dekker (Eds.), *The Cambridge handbook of formal semantics* (pp. 3–32). Cambridge: Cambridge University Press.

Partee, B. H., ter Meulen, A. G., & Wall, R. (1990). Mathematical methods in linguistics (Vol. 30). *Studies in Linguistics and Philosophy.* Dordrecht, NL: Kluwer Academic Press.

Pelletier, F. J. (1994). The principle of semantic compositionality. *Topoi, 13*(1), 11–24.

Pelletier, F. J. (2016). Semantic compositionality. In M. Aronoff (Ed.), *Oxford research encyclopedia of linguistics.* Oxford: Oxford University Press.

Perek, F. (2016). Using distributional semantics to study syntactic productivity in diachrony: A case study. *Linguistics, 54*(1), 149–188. https://doi.org/10.1515/ling-2015-0043.

Perek, F. (2018). Recent change in the productivity and schematicity of the way-construction: A distributional semantic analysis. *Corpus Linguistics and Linguistic Theory, 14*(1), 65–97.

Pickering, M. J., & Gambi, C. (2018). Predicting while comprehending language: A theory and review. *Psychological Bulletin, 144*(10), 1002–1044.

Pickering, M. J., & Garrod, S. (2013). An integrated theory of language production and comprehension. *Behavioral and Brain Sciences, 36*(4), 329–347.

Pinker, S. (1999). *Words and rules.* New York: Basic Books.

Pinker, S., & Prince, A. (1988). On language and connectionism: Analysis of a parallel distributed processing model of language acquisition. *Cognition, 28*(1–2), 73–193.

Pleyer, M., Lepic, R., & Hartmann, S. (2022). Compositionality in different modalities: A view from usage-based linguistics. *International Journal of Primatology, 45*, 670–702. https://doi.org/10.1007/s10764-022-00330-x.

Pullum, G. K., & Scholz, B. C. (2010). Recursion and the infinitude claim. *Recursion in Human Language, 104*, 111–138.

Pustejovsky, J. (1995). *The generative lexicon.* New York: MIT Press.

Pustejovsky, J. (2012). Co-compositionality in grammar. In W. Hinzen, E. Machery, & M. Werning (Eds.), *The Oxford handbook of compositionality* (pp. 371–382). Oxford; New York: Oxford University Press. https://doi.org/10.1093/oxfordhb/9780199541072.013.0017.

Pustejovsky, J., & Batiukova, O. (2019). *The lexicon.* Cambridge: Cambridge University Press.

Rambelli, G., Chersoni, E., Blache, P., Huang, C.- R., & Lenci, A. (2019). Distributional semantics meets construction grammar. Towards a unified usage-based model of grammar and meaning. In *Proceedings of the first international workshop on designing meaning representations (DMR 2019)* (pp. 110–120).

Rambelli, G., Chersoni, E., Blache, P., & Lenci, A. (2022). Compositionality as an analogical process: Introducing ANNE. In *Proceedings of the workshop on cognitive aspects of the lexicon* (pp. 78–96). Taipei: Association for Computational Linguistics.

Reed, S. E., Zhang, Y., Zhang, Y., & Lee, H. (2015). Deep visual analogy-making. In C. Cortes, N. Lawrence, D. Lee, M. Sugiyama, & R. Garnett (Eds.), *Advances in neural information processing systems* (Vol. 28, pp. 1252–1260). New York: Curran Associates.

Rimell, L., Maillard, J., Polajnar, T., & Clark, S. (2016). Relpron: A relative clause evaluation data set for compositional distributional semantics. *Computational Linguistics*, *42*(4), 661–701.

Rommers, J., Meyer, A. S., Praamstra, P., & Huettig, F. (2013). The contents of predictions in sentence comprehension: Activation of the shape of objects before they are referred to. *Neuropsychologia*, *51*(3), 437–447.

Sadeghi, F., Zitnick, C. L., & Farhadi, A. (2015). Visalogy: Answering visual analogy questions. In C. Cortes, N. Lawrence, D. Lee, M. Sugiyama & R. Garnett (Eds.), *Proceedings of the 28th International Conference on Neural Information Processing Systems* (Vol. 2, pp. 1882–1890). Montreal: MIT Press.

Sag, I. A. (2010). English filler-gap constructions. *Language*, *86*(3), 486–545.

Sag, I. A. (2012). Sign-based construction grammar: An informal synopsis. In H. C. Boas & I. A. Sag (Eds.), *Sign-based construction grammar* (Vol. 193, pp. 69–202). Stanford: CSLI.

Sag, I. A., Boas, H. C., & Kay, P. (2012). Introducing sign-based construction grammar. In H. C. Boas & I. A. Sag (Eds.), *Sign-based construction grammar* (pp. 1–29). Standford: CSLI.

Sag, I. A., & Pollard, C. (1994). *Head-driven phrase structure grammar.* Chicago, IL: University of Chicago Press.

Sahlgren, M. (2008). The distributional hypothesis. *Italian Journal of Disability Studies*, 33–53.

Sampson, G. (2016). Two ideas of creativity. In M. Hinton (Eds.), Evidence, experiment and argument in linguistics and the philosophy of language (pp. 15–26). Berlin: Peter Lang Verlag.

Sanford, A. J. (2002). Context, attention and depth of processing during interpretation. *Mind & Language, 17*(1–2), 188–206.

Sanford, A. J., & Sturt, P. (2002). Depth of processing in language comprehension: Not noticing the evidence. *Trends in Cognitive Sciences, 6*(9), 382–386.

Senaldi, M. S. G., & Titone, D. (2022). Less direct, more analytical: Eye-movement measures of L2 idiom reading. *Languages, 7*(2), 91.

Senaldi, M. S. G., & Titone, D. (2024). Idiom meaning selection following a prior context: Eye movement evidence of l1 direct retrieval and l2 compositional assembly. *Discourse Processes, 61*, 1–23. https://doi.org/10.1080/0163853X.2024.2311637.

Senaldi, M. S. G., Wei, J., Gullifer, J. W., & Titone, D. (2022). Scratching your Tête over language-switched idioms: Evidence from eye-movement measures of reading. *Memory & Cognition, 50*(6), 1230–1256.

Shieber, S. M., & Pereira, F. C. (1987). *Prolog and natural-language analysis.* Center for the Study of Language and Information.

Siyanova-Chanturia, A., Conklin, K., & Schmitt, N. (2011). Adding more fuel to the fire: An eye-tracking study of idiom processing by native and non-native speakers. *Second Language Research, 27*(2), 251–272.

Siyanova-Chanturia, A., & Sidtis, D. V. L. (2018). What online processing tells us about formulaic language. In A. Siyanova-Chanturia and A. Pellicer-Sánchez (Eds.), *Understanding formulaic language* (pp. 38–61). New York: Routledge.

Skousen, R. (1989). *Analogical modeling of language.* Dordrecht: Springer Science & Business Media.

Skousen, R. (1992). *Analogy and structure.* Dordrecht: Springer Science & Business Media.

Snider, N., & Arnon, I. (2012). A unified lexicon and grammar? Compositional and non-compositional phrases in the lexicon. In D. Divjak & S. Gries (Eds.), *Volume 2 frequency effects in language representation* (pp. 127–164). Berlin: De Gruyter Mouton. https://doi.org/10.1515/9783110274073.127.

Socher, R., Huval, B., Manning, C. D., & Ng, A. Y. (2012). Semantic compositionality through recursive matrix-vector spaces. In *Proceedings of the 2012 joint conference on empirical methods in natural language processing and computational natural language learning* (pp. 1201–1211).

Socher, R., Manning, C. D., & Ng, A. Y. (2010). Learning continuous phrase representations and syntactic parsing with recursive neural networks. In *Proceedings of the NIPS2010 deep learning and unsupervised feature learning workshop* (pp. 1–9).

Socher, R., Perelygin, A., Wu, J., et al. (2013). Recursive deep models for semantic compositionality over a sentiment treebank. In *Proceedings of the 2013 conference on empirical methods in natural language processing* (pp. 1631–1642).

Staub, A., & Clifton, C. J. (2006). Syntactic prediction in language comprehension: Evidence from either... or. *Journal of Experimental Psychology: Learning, Memory, and Cognition, 32*, 425–436.

Steedman, M. (2001). *The syntactic process*. Cambridge, MA: MIT press.

Steels, L. (2011). Introducing Fluid Construction Grammar. In L. Steels (Ed.), *Design patterns in fluid construction grammar* (pp. 3–30). Amsterdam: John Benjamins Publishing Company. https://doi.org/10.1075/cal.11.03ste.

Steels, L. (2013). Fluid construction grammar. In T. Hoffmann & G. Trousdale (Eds.), *The Oxford handbook of construction grammar* (pp. 153–167). Oxford: Oxford University Press. https://doi.org/10.1093/oxfordhb/9780195396683.013.0009.

Steels, L. (2017). Basics of fluid construction grammar. *Constructions and Frames, 9*(2), 178–225. https://doi.org/10.1075/cf.00002.ste.

Swinney, D. A., & Cutler, A. (1979). The access and processing of idiomatic expressions. *Journal of Verbal Learning and Verbal Behavior, 18*(5), 523–534.

Szabó, Z. G. (2000). Compositionality as supervenience. *Linguistics and Philosophy, 23*, 475–505.

Szabó, Z. G. (2012). The case for compositionality. In W. Hinzen, M. Werning, & E. Machery (Eds.), *The Oxford handbook of compositionality* (pp. 64–80). New York: Oxford University Press.

Tabossi, P., Fanari, R., & Wolf, K. (2009). Why are idioms recognized fast? *Memory & Cognition, 37*(4), 529–540.

Tanenhaus, M. K., Spivey-Knowlton, M. J., Eberhard, K. M., & Sedivy, J. C. (1995). Integration of visual and linguistic information in spoken language comprehension. *Science, 268*(5217), 1632–1634.

Titone, D., Columbus, G., Whitford, V., Mercier, J., & Libben, M. (2015). Contrasting bilingual and monolingual idiom processing. In R. R. Heredia & A. B. Cieślicka (Eds.), *Bilingual figurative language processing* (pp. 171–207). Cambridge: Cambridge University Press.

Titone, D., & Connine, C. M. (1999). On the compositional and noncompositional nature of idiomatic expressions. *Journal of Pragmatics, 31*(12), 1655–1674.

Tomasello, M. (2009). *Constructing a language: A usage-based theory of language acquisition*. Cambridge, MA: Harvard University Press.

Tremblay, A., & Baayen, R. H. (2010). Holistic processing of regular four-word sequences: A behavioral and ERP study of the effects of structure, frequency, and probability on immediate free recall. In D. Wood (Ed.), *Perspectives on formulaic language: Acquisition and communication* (pp. 151–173). London: Continuum.

Tremblay, A., Derwing, B., Libben, G., & Westbury, C. (2011). Processing advantages of lexical bundles: Evidence from self-paced reading and sentence recall tasks. *Language Learning, 61*(2), 569–613.

Turner, M. (2018). The role of creativity in multimodal construction grammar. *Zeitschrift für Anglistik und Amerikanistik, 66*(3), 357–370. https://doi.org/10.1515/zaa-2018-0030.

Ungerer, T., & Hartmann, S. (2020). Delineating extravagance: Assessing speakers' perceptions of imaginative constructional patterns. *Belgian Journal of Linguistics. 34*(1), 345–356. https://doi.org/10.1075/bjl.00058.ung.

Ungerer, T., & Hartmann, S. (2023). *Constructionist approaches: Past, present, future*. Cambridge: Cambridge University Press. https://doi.org/10.1017/9781009308717.

Upchurch, P., Snavely, N., & Bala, K. (2016). From a to z: Supervised transfer of style and content using deep neural network generators. *arXiv preprint arXiv:1603.02003*.

Ushio, A., Espinosa Anke, L., Schockaert, S., & Camacho-Collados, J. (2021, August). BERT is to NLP what AlexNet is to CV: Can pre-trained language models identify analogies? In *Proceedings of the 59th annual meeting of the association for computational linguistics and the 11th international joint conference on natural language processing (volume 1: Long papers)* (pp. 3609–3624). Online: Association for Computational Linguistics.

Vespignani, F., Canal, P., Molinaro, N., Fonda, S., & Cacciari, C. (2010). Predictive mechanisms in idiom comprehension. *Journal of Cognitive Neuroscience, 22*(8), 1682–1700.

Wang, Y., Daille, B., & Hathout, N. (2021). Caractérisation des relations sémantiques entre termes multi-mots fondée sur l'analogie (semantic relations recognition between multi-word terms by means of analogy). In *Actes de la 28e conférence sur le traitement automatique des langues naturelles. volume 1 : conférence principale* (pp. 115–124). ATALA.

Wray, A. (2002). *Formulaic language and the lexicon*. Cambridge: Cambridge University Press.

Wray, A. (2012). What do we (think we) know about formulaic language? An evaluation of the current state of play. *Annual Review of Applied Linguistics, 32*, 231–254.

Zanzotto, F. M., Korkontzelos, I., Fallucchi, F., & Manandhar, S. (2010). Estimating linear models for compositional distributional semantics. In *International conference on computational linguistics (coling)*.

Zhu, X., & de Melo, G. (2020). Sentence analogies: Linguistic regularities in sentence embeddings. In *Proceedings of the 28th international conference on computational linguistics* (pp. 3389–3400).

Acknowledgments

I thank Alex Bergs and Thomas Hoffmann, the series editors, for having faith in me and for providing support and positive feedback in the reviewing months. I'm also thankful for the comments by an anonymous reviewer, which helped me sharpen the focus of this manuscript.

This Element comes from a part of my PhD thesis, which I could not have done without the support and guidance of my supervisors, Alessandro Lenci and Philippe Blache. I am also grateful to all the people who reviewed my original thesis, Professors Giosué Baggio, Florent Perek, Adele Goldberg, and Aline Villavicencio. They have inspired me with their research, and I was honored they evaluated mine. I also thank Marianna Bolognesi for giving me the time to write these pages during my postdoc.

Cambridge Elements ☰

Construction Grammar

Thomas Hoffmann
Catholic University of Eichstätt-Ingolstadt

Thomas Hoffmann is Full Professor and Chair of English Language and Linguistics at the Catholic University of Eichstätt-Ingolstadt as well as Furong Scholar Distinguished Chair Professor of Hunan Normal University. His main research interests are usage-based Construction Grammar, language variation and change and linguistic creativity. He has published widely in international journals such as *Cognitive Linguistics*, *English Language and Linguistics*, and *English World-Wide*. His monographs *Preposition Placement in English* (2011) and *English Comparative Correlatives: Diachronic and Synchronic Variation at the Lexicon-Syntax Interface* (2019) were both published by Cambridge University Press. His textbook on *Construction Grammar: The Structure of English* (2022) as well as an Element on *The Cognitive Foundation of Post-colonial Englishes: Construction Grammar as the Cognitive Theory for the Dynamic Model* (2021) have also both been published with Cambridge University Press. He is also co-editor (with Graeme Trousdale) of *The Oxford Handbook of Construction Grammar* (2013, Oxford University Press).

Alexander Bergs
Osnabrück University

Alexander Bergs joined the Institute for English and American Studies at Osnabrück University, Germany, in 2006 when he became Full Professor and Chair of English Language and Linguistics. His research interests include, among others, language variation and change, constructional approaches to language, the role of context in language, the syntax/pragmatics interface, and cognitive poetics. His works include several authored and edited books (*Social Networks and Historical Sociolinguistics*, *Modern Scots*, *Contexts and Constructions*, *Constructions and Language Change*), a short textbook on *Synchronic English Linguistics*, one on *Understanding Language Change* (with Kate Burridge) and the two-volume *Handbook of English Historical Linguistics* (ed. with Laurel Brinton; now available as five-volume paperback) as well as more than fifty papers in high-profile international journals and edited volumes. Alexander Bergs has taught at the Universities of Düsseldorf, Bonn, Santiago de Compostela, Wisconsin-Milwaukee, Catania, Vigo, Thessaloniki, Athens, and Dalian and has organized numerous international workshops and conferences.

About the Series

Construction Grammar is the leading cognitive theory of syntax. The present Elements series will survey its theoretical building blocks, show how Construction Grammar can capture various linguistic phenomena across a wide range of typologically different languages, and identify emerging frontier topics from a theoretical, empirical and applied perspective.

Cambridge Elements ⊟

Construction Grammar

Elements in the Series

Printed in the United States
by Baker & Taylor Publisher Services